the
ultimate
film
guides

Trainspotting

Director
Danny Boyle

Note by Martin Stollery

gman

York Press

York Press
322 Old Brompton Road, London SW5 9JH

Pearson Education Limited
Edinburgh Gate, Harlow, Essex CM20 2JE, United Kingdom
Associated companies, branches and representatives throughout
the world

First published 2001

ISBN 0-582-45258-9

Designed by Vicki Pacey
Phototypeset by Gem Graphics, Trenance, Mawgan Porth, Cornwall
Colour reproduction and film output by Spectrum Colour
Produced by Addison Wesley Longman China Limited, Hong Kong

contents

dedication

This book is for Helen Eyers.

—///—

author of this note Martin Stollery is Senior Lecturer in Film Studies in the Faculty of Media, Arts and Society at Southampton Institute. Publications include *Alternative Empires: European Modernist Cinemas and Cultures of Imperialism* (Exeter University Press, 2000), *L'Emigré* (Flicks Books, 2001) and *York Film Notes: Lawrence of Arabia* (York Press, 2000) He is currently co-authoring a book on British film editors.

background

trailer

British cinematic culture has a very strong tradition of dogged realism, and that's something we fought against. We didn't want [*Trainspotting*] to be the kind of drug film that has a lot of bleak shots of housing estates as its context. The book is about the spirit within the characters, which is what we tried to capture. It's meant to be from [the addict's] point of view, rather than that of outsiders who don't do heroin.

Danny Boyle, quoted in Andrew O. Thompson, 'Trains, Veins and Heroin Deals',
American Cinematographer vol.77 no.8, August 1996

Stringing itself out on little hits of sensation ...

Tom Shone, The Sunday Times, 25 February 1996

The rollercoaster rush of an unforgettable first half hour [gives way to] a sudden and shocking reality injection ... it's a stunning turnaround.

Neil Jeffries, Empire, September 1996

A gleeful repertoire of frozen frames, card-shuffling montage sequences, queasy false perspectives, and fantastical visual punctuation.

Harlan Kennedy, 'Kiltspotting: Highland Reels', Film Comment vol.32 no.4,
July-August 1996

White socks ... essential wear for nutters!

Robert Carlyle (on Begbie's clothes), quoted in The Face, February 1996

Polygram is marketing *Trainspotting* as the next cult hit with crossover appeal.

Alice Rawsthorn, Financial Times, 27 January 1996

important for a youth audience

> The film is true to the book in the sense that it carries no moral message about the lives of its characters or the drugs they use.
>
> Susan Corrigan, ID, February 1996

> As with all great movies it defies easy classification ... *Trainspotting* has become a film synonymous with nineties British culture.
>
> Xan Brooks, 'Choose Life: Ewan McGregor and the British Film Revival', 1998

reading trainspotting

In 1999, the BFI (British Film Institute) compiled a list of the hundred best British films of all time. *Trainspotting* came tenth. It was the highest placed British film of the 1990s, followed by *Four Weddings and a Funeral* (Mike Newell, 1994) at twenty-three and *The Full Monty* (Peter Cattaneo, 1997) at twenty-five. In future years, *Trainspotting* may fall lower down this list but it is fairly safe to bet it will probably remain the highest placed film of the 1990s. It therefore deserves serious critical attention.

Trainspotting's lead in the top one hundred over other successful 1990s' British films relates to a widespread perception that it broke new ground in a number of ways. Not everyone would agree with the value judgement underlying *Time Out* reviewer Tom Charity's declaration that '*Trainspotting* is the movie we have all been waiting for'. Most commentators, however, would agree that *Trainspotting* crystallised important new stylistic, cultural and industrial trends within British cinema of the 1990s (see Contexts: Industrial and Filmography). *Trainspotting*'s appeal was wide-ranging but it was particularly targeted at and especially important for a youth audience.

Trainspotting is about a group of young men, most of whom are heroin addicts. Its playful style distinguishes it from the realist approach one might expect of a British film dealing with this subject matter. British cinema has a long tradition of realist film making. This includes 'New Wave' classics such as *Saturday Night and Sunday Morning* (Karel Reisz, 1960) and more recent films directed by Ken Loach, Mike Leigh and others. These films focus on working or lower middle-class characters and employ a particular style to achieve an impression of realism (see Style: Cinematography). In interviews, Andrew Macdonald, John Hodge and Danny Boyle, the leading members of *Trainspotting*'s production team, talked about how and why they purposefully departed from British cinema's 'very strong tradition of dogged realism'.

Trainspotting's adventurous but accessible style and the high profile marketing campaign which promoted the film helped it attract wide audiences. Claire Monk, in her essay 'Underbelly UK: the 1990s underclass film, masculinity and the ideologies of 'new Britain'', explores some cultural contexts for *Trainspotting*'s success. She identifies a number of what she calls 1990s' 'underclass' films which relate to yet depart from the British realist tradition. They belong to different genres and are targeted at different audiences but there are significant similarities between them. They were by no means the only type of films produced during this period, but they were among the most successful. These underclass films represent unemployed and socially excluded groups of men but make this subject matter enjoyable through comedy and style.

The Full Monty, for example, is a film shot in a realist style about a group of unemployed Sheffield men. What was novel about the film's treatment of this material and what attracted record audiences was its feel-good comedy. The men deal with their initially low self-esteem by bonding together and creating work for themselves as strippers. In *The Full Monty*, difficult social and economic problems are resolved through male bonding and humour. *Trainspotting* does not represent its characters' situation as a social problem which they are victims of or must struggle against. Its style steers away from the 'bleak shots of housing estates' that director Danny Boyle associates with British realist films. Instead, it attempts to capture 'the spirit within the characters' (see Narrative & Form: Narration: Restricted Narration). Certain aspects of how the characters experience their lifestyle are represented as appealing (see Style: Production Design and Cinematography).

Monk links the particular emphasis on all-male groups in these films to wider trends in representations of masculinity in 1990s' British culture (see Cultural Contexts: New Lads). She also relates these films to 'Cool

an undertow of meaninglessness

Britannia' and the project of 're-branding Britain' which took off in the mid-1990s. The media attention given to Britpop, new British art and fashion during the 1990s, generated perceptions of British culture as creative and dynamic. The term 'Cool Britannia' was coined in 1996 to encapsulate this. *Trainspotting* was incorporated under this banner as the most stylish example of new British cinema. The new Labour government elected in 1997 pushed this trend further. It committed itself to re-branding Britain by encouraging the promotion of new images of the nation as culturally diverse, classless, modern, energetic and most importantly of all, enterprising.

Trainspotting and *The Full Monty* are set in diverse areas of Britain. Both films revise older images of the areas they are set in and represent their local cultures as fully in tune with modern times (see Cultural Contexts: Representing Scotland). Both films represent creative, enterprising characters who eventually leave the underclass to achieve business success. The men in *The Full Monty* stage their strip show to a club full of eager punters who pay good money to see them. Renton in *Trainspotting* becomes an estate agent in London and then the main beneficiary of a drug deal. *Trainspotting*'s narrative structure infuses Renton's achievements with an undertow of meaninglessness, but the film certainly does not represent any positive alternatives to the ideology of the enterprise culture (see Narrative & Form: Opening/Close and Contexts: Ideology: Post-Thatcherism).

Monk concludes her analysis by criticising the assumption in these films that leaving the underclass is primarily a matter of individual choice. For her, this is an ideological assumption which should be challenged. In her view these films prevent further exploration of factors preventing people from leaving the underclass. They ignore the deep-rooted causes of economic and social inequalities. They deny the need to think about radical, collective solutions to these problems.

Monk's analysis is useful for the way it can be used to raise quite specific questions about *Trainspotting*. One example is the **montage sequence** which magically transports Renton from an underclass life in Edinburgh to an enterprising one in London. The **ellipsis** this creates within the narrative avoids the need to represent any difficulties Renton might have encountered in making a transition from unemployment to employment and from one social class to another (see Narrative & Form: Space).

Danny Boyle, discussing *Trainspotting* in a *Sight and Sound* interview, expressed a different view of these issues. He argued the 'interesting thing about class [is] your own private relationship with it, what you do with it. Not just 'it' as a monumental force controlling everyone.' Boyle's view was more in tune with dominant political and cultural thinking in the 1990s. This was a period where the radical left-wing perspectives underpinning Monk's analysis were out of fashion (see Contexts: Ideology: Post-Thatcherism).

key players' biographies

PRODUCER: ANDREW MACDONALD

Trainspotting's producer, Andrew Macdonald, started at the bottom of the film industry and worked his way up to producer. His grandfather, Emeric Pressburger, collaborated with director Michael Powell on a series of outstanding films during the 1940s and 1950s. Macdonald began as a runner, the person who does odd jobs while a film is in production. Subsequent employment included script reading and location managing. He worked at Palace Pictures with film producer Steve Woolley. Macdonald gained useful experience working in different capacities on different types of British film production. These ranged from the costly, unsuccessful epic *Revolution* (Hugh Hudson, 1985) to more modestly-budgeted films such as *The Big Man* (David Leland, 1990) and *The Long Day Closes* (Terence Davies, 1992).

Macdonald's grandfather's best work emerged from his collaboration with Michael Powell. Macdonald's core team – consisting of himself, screenwriter John Hodge and director Danny Boyle – have shown a similar commitment to long-term collaboration. Macdonald met Hodge in the early 1990s and read an early draft of his original screenplay, *Shallow Grave*. David Aukin, Channel 4's head of drama, supported the project and Boyle was recruited as director. *Shallow Grave* scored a critical and a remix of his novel

commercial success. The team stayed together for *Trainspotting*, *A Life Less Ordinary* (Danny Boyle, 1997) and *The Beach* (Danny Boyle, 2000). Production teams who stay together tend to develop ways of communicating which help them work through potential conflicts and collaborate efficiently. This helps the producer keep the production on schedule and within budget.

Producers access sources of production finance, assemble production teams and steer projects through to completion. With *Trainspotting*, it was Macdonald who initiated the project by encouraging Hodge and Boyle to read the Irvine Welsh novel the film is based upon. Once the project was underway, Macdonald's responsibilities as *Trainspotting*'s producer involved liaising with Polygram, the film's distributors, working on publicity and obtaining permission to use all the music included on the soundtrack (see Contexts: Production History). At the outset Macdonald also had to secure the rights to Irvine Welsh's source novel. Protracted negotiations were necessary to obtain the screen rights because the book's publishers had already sold them to another production company.

THE AUTHOR: IRVINE WELSH

Author Irvine Welsh, author of *Trainspotting* the novel, was supportive of the *Trainspotting* film. His novel consists of numerous short episodes featuring different sets of characters. It was partly developed through combining versions of short stories and sketches Welsh had already published elsewhere. *Trainspotting* the novel was a great success and some readers were concerned about whether a film version would remain true to their understanding of the book. Welsh's attitude towards the film helped defuse such sentiments. He never expected the film makers to produce a faithful adaptation of his novel. Instead, he used an analogy for the adaptation process which was very apposite for a film where music is so crucial (see Style: Music). He talked in interviews about his enthusiasm for the film as a cover version or remix of his novel.

SCREENWRITER'S ADAPTATION: JOHN HODGE

John Hodge was a newcomer to adapting novels when he started work on the *Trainspotting* screenplay. Before starting to write, he discussed with

Andrew Macdonald and Danny Boyle what they liked about the novel, which aspects they should keep and which they could dispense with. The novel's representation of the pleasures as well as the negative consequences of heroin use struck a chord with the *Trainspotting* production team, but they also emphasised that the book and the film were about more than this.

Hodge said of *Trainspotting*: 'It's a film about a bunch of guys. I wanted to reflect the lives, the attitude, the characters and the language that are all depicted in the book' (Macnab, *Sight and Sound*, February 1996). Macdonald commented: 'John Hodge manages to twist it round to his agenda ... He managed to make it about friendship and betrayal.' Friendship and betrayal is an important theme in *Shallow Grave* and *The Beach*. In *Shallow Grave*, like *Trainspotting*, friendships break down over the unexpected arrival of a large sum of money.

Hodge's objective was to hone *Trainspotting* the novel's sprawling narrative into a film lasting approximately ninety minutes. Yet he did not want to depart too radically from the novel. Otherwise, as he put it, 'what's the point in buying the rights? You could buy a blank page for nothing.' *Trainspotting* the film is more streamlined than *Trainspotting* the novel. The film features fewer characters. Whereas there are several episodes in the novel that the protagonist Renton does not appear in, he is more central to the film's narrative (see Narrative & Form: Narration: Restricted Narration). Nevertheless, the film retains some of the novel's episodic nature (see Narrative & Form: Little Hits of Sensation and Character). As a narrative device, Renton's voice-over in the film is broadly equivalent to his **interior monologue** in the novel (see Narrative & Form: Narration: Voice-over).

Adapting *Trainspotting* involved expanding and transforming as well as eliminating and finding equivalents for aspects of the novel. Renton's and Spud's shoplifting spree, briefly referred to in the novel, is directly represented twice in the film (see Narrative & Form: Chronology). The film opens with shots of Renton and Spud running down Edinburgh's Princes Street being chased by security guards. This instantly establishes the film's dynamic pace and style. Lines of dialogue from the novel are sometimes transposed into contexts where film adds another dimension to them. In the novel, Renton is in a pub when he outlines his feelings about being Scottish. In the film, this takes place against the background of a magnificent landscape (see Contexts: Cultural Contexts: Representing Scotland).

One compelling aspect of *Trainspotting* the novel is the stylised vernacular used by the characters. The voice-over in the film adapts many lines from Irvine Welsh's novel but omits some of their slang and vernacular phrasings (see Narrative & Form: Narration: Voice-over). Novel readers can work at their own pace to decipher characters' speech, but at a cinema screening, lines of dialogue and monologue can only be heard once. The language in *Trainspotting* the film is rich and vibrant but more accessible than in the novel.

Many cultural references specific to Scotland and Edinburgh are excised from the film for the same reason. The novel addresses tensions between Protestants and Catholics, discrimination based on educational background and local football rivalries. The film contains fewer specific cultural references and when they do occur they are less prominent than in the book. Spud briefly garbles about different Edinburgh schools at the beginning of his job interview, but the speed of his delivery and the **jump cuts** linking these shots are more perceptible than the content of his dialogue (see Style: Editing). Renton has a Hibs rosette and banner in his bedroom and praises Scottish striker Archie Gemmill, but these are incidental details. Locations such as Princes Street and the Volcano club, a famous Glasgow night spot, are represented in the film but the predominance of stylised interior spaces makes it less culturally specific than the novel (see Style: Production Design).

There are quite a few explicit historical and political references in Renton's dialogue and interior monologue in *Trainspotting* the novel but very few in *Trainspotting* the film. At various points in the novel's narrative, Renton reflects upon issues such as: the conflict in Northern Ireland; the consequences of mass unemployment and government housing policy; and the relationship between profits from investment and economic deprivation in other parts of the world. *Trainspotting* the novel is neither a historical analysis nor a political critique of the circumstances surrounding heroin use in Edinburgh, but these reflections do supply a wider context to its narrative. Hodge's adaptation removes all of this.

Bert Cardullo, in his essay 'Fiction into Film, or Bringing Welsh to a Boyle', explores the differences between the beginning and end of *Trainspotting* the novel and *Trainspotting* the film. The novel begins with Renton and Sick Boy watching a Jean-Claude Van Damme video. It ends with Renton on a boat to Amsterdam, contemplating the terrifying and exciting possibility that now he could be what he wanted to be. The film is less certain about the prospect of achieving change and personal development through moving to another, possibly better place (see Narrative & Form: Space).

Trainspotting the film's narrative begins and ends with Renton's voice-over reciting versions of the now famous 'choose life' monologue. This is adapted from the novel, where it appears half way through the narrative in an episode entitled 'Searching for the Inner Man'. In this episode, Renton rejects, through the 'choose life' interior monologue, the consumerism and conventional lifestyle society has to offer. In the film, Renton's voice-over similarly rejects this at the beginning of the narrative but seems to accept it at the end. However, the tone of Renton's voice-over and the composition of the final shot of him at the end of the film ends the narrative ambiguously. The film's ending raises questions about whether it is possible for Renton to make a positive, meaningful choice (see Narrative & Form: Opening/Close).

PRODUCTION AND COSTUME DESIGNERS

Trainspotting's distinctive visual style derived partly from director Danny Boyle's preference for filming within controlled environments. Much of *Trainspotting* was shot on sets built inside an abandoned cigarette factory in Glasgow. This enabled the production team, as Boyle put it, to 'create our own universe ... we can work any way we like in terms of colour, light, space and movement'. Boyle assembled a large scrapbook of images in order to communicate to his collaborators the kind of look he was searching for.

a visual indication of disorganised lifestyle

Production designer Kave Quinn, who also worked on *Shallow Grave*, developed the look of the film. Different parts of Swanney's drug den, the main setting in the earlier part of *Trainspotting*'s narrative, were painted in a range of seductive colours. This stylised approach to production design differs from the location shooting favoured by realist film makers (see Style: Production Design and Cinematography). Boyle and Quinn have acknowledged the influence of films directed by Pedro Almodovar and Peter Greenaway which use colour in a similar way. *The Cook, the Thief, his Wife and her Lover* (Peter Greenaway, 1989), for example, is set in a restaurant where each room is a different, eye-catching colour.

Quinn and art director Tracey Gallacher collected many items which form part of *Trainspotting*'s mise-en-scène: for example the cylindrical floor lamps in Swanney's drug den and the bottles and other bric-a-brac which litter the floor. The minimal furnishing in the den and the eclectic items on the floor provide an immediate visual indication of the characters' disorganised lifestyle. Costume designer Rachael Fleming assembled the characters' outfits from diverse sources such as charity shops and production crew members' old clothes. It was particularly important for a film targeted at a youth audience to achieve an effective blend of 1980s' and 1990s' fashions (see Style: Fashion and Contexts: Production History).

CINEMATOGRAPHER: BRIAN TUFANO

Cinematographer Brian Tufano was one of the most experienced members of the *Trainspotting* production team. His career demonstrates considerable versatility, encompassing documentaries and television mini-series. His work on feature films includes the cult youth film *Quadrophenia* (Franc Roddam, 1979), realist comedies and dramas such as *East is East* (Damien O'Donnell, 1999) and *Billy Elliot* (Stephen Daldry, 2000) as well as *Shallow Grave* and *A Life Less Ordinary* with Danny Boyle in the mid-1990s. *Shallow Grave* pioneered Tufano's distinctive, flamboyant style of cinematography for Boyle. This style, involving primary-coloured lighting, unusual camera angles and occasional rapid camera movements, was developed further in *Trainspotting*.

Coloured gel on windows, **practicals** and **off–screen fixtures** helped achieve the yellow, green, red and blue tones in different rooms within Swanney's drug den (see Style: Production Design). Tufano's work on *Trainspotting* extended techniques from *Shallow Grave* by employing shots taken from diverse angles, **impossible camera positions**, and often from a low height. Improvisation was sometimes necessary to film these. One example is the fast moving ground level **tracking shots** of Renton running down Edinburgh's Princes Street. These were taken by Tufano operating a lightweight camera, lying flat on a motorcycle sidecar attachment moving alongside Ewan McGregor. They form part of a recurring pattern throughout *Trainspotting* of shots taken from a low **camera height** (see Style: Cinematography).

EDITOR: MASAHIRO HIRAKUBO

Editor Masahiro Hirakubo was another key member of the *Trainspotting* production team. He also edited *Shallow Grave*, *A Life Less Ordinary* and *The Beach*. He was central to the process of coordinating *Trainspotting*'s images, voice-over and music and sustaining the film's dynamic pace. Hirakubo's editing lends many of *Trainspotting*'s sequences a music video feel, and there are many playful editing experiments scattered throughout the film (see Narrative & Form: Little Hits Of Sensation and Style: Editing).

Over and above specific experiments, Hirakubo's creative input was crucial to giving shape and coherence to the film as a whole. He felt that in this respect *Trainspotting* was 'quite a difficult project to edit because it doesn't have a proper narrative flow, which means that one scene won't necessarily relate to the next. Also it has a lot of music ...' (Westbrook, *Empire*, March 1996). *Trainspotting*'s narrative structure is indebted to music video and the traditions of art cinema (see Narrative & Form: Little Hits Of Sensation and Art Cinema Influences). In music videos and art cinema, sequences are internally organised and linked in ways which differ from conventional, tightly-plotted, flowing narratives (see Narrative & Form: Character and Chronology). This requires an approach to editing which is different from that employed in more conventional films.

full frontal nudity

EWAN MCGREGOR

Trainspotting's success boosted the careers of the leading actors involved in the film. Ewan McGregor went on to secure the role of Obi-Wan Kenobi in *Star Wars: Episode I – The Phantom Menace* (George Lucas, 1999) and further prequels. Prior to *Trainspotting*, McGregor appeared in *Shallow Grave* as a relatively unknown film actor. Both *Shallow Grave*'s and *Trainspotting*'s endings use McGregor's face in similar ways. In *Shallow Grave*, McGregor's character ends pinned to a carpet by a knife, smiling because of the pile of money stashed below him under the floorboards. He also smiles in the final shot of him in *Trainspotting* (see Narrative & Form: Opening/Close). In both films, McGregor plays an articulate, devious yet likeable character who betrays friends to achieve an ambiguous triumph. Later films such as *Rogue Trader* (James Dearden, 1999) build upon these aspects of McGregor's star image.

Sarah Street, in her book *British Cinema in Documents*, analyses McGregor's star image in detail. One aspect she highlights is McGregor's reputation for full frontal nudity in film and stage performances. This is taken to an extreme in *Velvet Goldmine* (Todd Haynes, 1998) and particularly *The Pillow Book* (Peter Greenaway, 1996) where McGregor's naked body is central to the film. He also appears naked in a sex scene in *Trainspotting*. This aspect of McGregor's image provides a clear point of appeal for fans. It is also of critical interest because it is relatively unusual for a male star's body to be so explicitly represented. Analysing the precise ways in which bodies are represented in film often reveals subtle differences based upon gender (see Style: Fashion and Contexts: Cultural Contexts: New Lads).

ROBERT CARLYLE

Robert Carlyle's career benefited from appearing as Begbie in *Trainspotting*. His policeman in the television series *Hamish Macbeth* (1995) and subsequent leading roles in *Carla's Song* (Ken Loach, 1996) and *The Full Monty* demonstrated versatility and the ability to play gentler characters. The violent, unpredictable, borderline psychotic criminal Carlyle played in the television series *Looking After Jo Jo* (1998) echoed Begbie in

Trainspotting. Carlyle's cannibal in *Ravenous* (Antonia Bird, 1999) and villain in the James Bond film *The World is Not Enough* (Michael Apted, 1999) further extended this aspect of his perceived persona. Carlyle's troubled gangster in *Face* (Antonia Bird, 1997) combines the violent and gentle strands of his star image. In *Trainspotting*, Carlyle's age, a decade older than McGregor, is one factor which marks Begbie as the least stylish and most problematic of Renton's friends (see Style: Fashion and Contexts: Cultural Contexts: New Lads).

EWEN BREMNER

Ewen Bremner fleshed out his role as Spud with a verbally inarticulate but physically energetic performance. It was his first major film role. Danny Boyle recognised the importance of organising the shooting in order to allow Bremner freedom to deliver this kind of performance. In the job interview sequence, the aim was to 'shoot it wide and he can jump about as much as he likes' (Macnab, *Sight and Sound*, February 1996). Editing also works in tandem with Bremner's performance in this sequence (see Style: Editing). Bremner as Spud is central to the slapstick comedy in the earlier part of *Trainspotting*'s narrative (see Narrative & Form: Little Hits Of Sensation and Character).

director as auteur

Prior to directing feature films, Danny Boyle worked in theatre before moving into television as a producer and director. Boyle, like Andrew Macdonald and John Hodge, is a keen admirer of the work of American independent film makers such as Martin Scorsese, Stanley Kubrick, Quentin Tarantino and the Coen brothers. All of these influences feed into and are sometimes explicitly referred to in his work (see Narrative & Form: Art Cinema Influences and Contexts: Genre).

Studying a director as an 'auteur' involves looking for thematic and stylistic consistencies and developments across the entire body of that individual director's film work. Boyle's skill and intelligence as a director is evident, but this approach cannot yet be applied to him because all of his feature

collective intentions and achievements

films have been made by the same core production team of himself, Macdonald and Hodge. When interviewed, they tend to speak of their collective intentions and achievements, and those of their other collaborators, rather than in terms of a uniquely personal vision. What is significant about the *Trainspotting* production team is that their work together highlights an issue which is not always fully acknowledged by film historians, critics and film makers: that collaboration is essential to all film making.

narrative & form

little hits of sensation

Trainspotting's opening five minutes establish the narrative's dynamic pace. Moving straight into action, the film dispenses with conventional credits. **Crosscutting** introduces five locations in the first five minutes (see Style: Editing): Shoplifters Renton and Spud are chased through the area around Edinburgh's Princes Street; Renton, Sick Boy, Begbie, Spud and Tommy play five-a-side football against the Calton Athletic team; characters inject heroin in different rooms in Swanney's drug den; Begbie and Tommy warn Renton about the dangers of heroin use across a pool table, as do Renton's parents at home. Key characters are identified by titles bearing their names. These are superimposed over brief **freeze frame** shots of them in arrested motion.

Trainspotting's production team limited the film's overall length to approximately ninety minutes in order to sustain narrative momentum. The narrative consists of many brief sequences. Momentum is sustained by moving quickly from one sequence to the next and not dwelling too long on any of them (see Style: Editing). These sequences are sometimes less than one and rarely more than three minutes long.

In the earlier part of the narrative, many sequences involve comic situations. These include Renton shooting an air rifle at a skinhead's dog in the park; Spud attending a job interview on speed; Renton stealing and watching a videotape of Tommy and Lizzy having sex; and the contents of Spud's soiled sheets being strewn around Gail's parents' breakfast room. The title of Will Self's review of *Trainspotting*, 'Carry on up the hypodermic' (1996), illustrates this aspect of the narrative structure. The title alludes to the popular British series of *Carry On* films whose narratives consist of a series of loosely connected comic turns.

little hits of sensation narrative & form

Trainspotting's soundtrack subdivides the narrative into sequences which resemble music videos (see Style: Music). There are several occasions in the narrative where a song, accompanied by stylish visual images, is played in its entirety. Iggy Pop's 'Lust for Life' during the opening five minutes is one example, Lou Reed's 'Perfect Day' is another. During 'Perfect Day', Renton overdoses at Swanney's drug den and imagines falling into the carpet. His trip to hospital is interspersed with **point-of-view shots** looking up from under the carpet (see Style: Cinematography). In the next sequence, Renton's parents lock him in his bedroom to come off heroin. Underworld's 'Dark and Long' pulsates continuously on the soundtrack during his vivid, jumbled hallucinations.

narration

RESTRICTED NARRATION

Trainspotting employs restricted narration throughout most of its narrative. This means that the range of what the **spectator** sees and knows is broadly restricted to Renton's range of vision, knowledge and imagination. Renton is directly involved in or is told about almost every event represented within the narrative. For example, he is the one character present in all five locations represented in *Trainspotting*'s opening sequence. In the few sequences where Renton is not present, the other characters' actions are usually commented on by his voice-over or compared to or related to him in some way (see Unrestricted Narration).

Restricted narration places Renton and the film's spectator on a relatively equal footing. The narrative does not allow the spectator to look down on him from a commanding position of superior knowledge. Restricted narration serves the production team's aim of representing heroin users, as Danny Boyle put it, 'from [the addict's] point of view, rather than that of outsiders' (Thompson, *American Cinematographer*, August 1996). Restricted narration places emphasis upon the subjective experience of this lifestyle rather than its social context.

Trainspotting does not place its characters within the wider context of a social problem which needs to be analysed and possibly remedied, as a more traditional British realist film might (see Background: Reading *Trainspotting*). Restricted narration, combined with fractured chronology, limits the possibility of directly relating Renton's situation to wider economic, political and social conflicts and processes (see Chronology). The narrative remains focused around Renton and his immediate group of friends who express little interest in such things (see Contexts: Ideology: Post-Thatcherism).

VOICE-OVER

Renton's voice-over opens and closes *Trainspotting*'s narrative and accompanies much of what happens in between. It is a structural device which serves several purposes:

■ Combined with restricted narration centred around Renton, it enables *Trainspotting*'s spectator to understand the film's stylised production design, cinematography and editing as, in part, an expression of his chemically altered consciousness (see Style: Production Design, Cinematography and Editing).

■ It helps impose a structure upon the little hits of sensation *Trainspotting*'s narrative consists of. The structure provided by the voice-over allows *Trainspotting*'s editing more freedom to be playful and audacious than would otherwise be the case (see Style: Editing).

■ It helps sustain the narrative's dynamic pace by quickly filling in any relevant information.

■ It maximises the narrative's intelligibility.

Trainspotting's voice-over, in conjunction with music, helps establish meaningful links between shots edited in a manner which might otherwise disorientate the spectator (see Style: Editing). For example, in the opening sequence, as Iggy Pop's 'Lust for Life' pounds on the soundtrack, Renton's voice-over declares you should choose good health. This phrase bridges a cut between two locations. It bridges a freeze frame shot, with a superimposed title identifying Renton, and the first shot of Swanney's drug den, where an unhealthy Renton begins to keel over. In the next shot, Renton's keeling over continues. His voice-over says you should choose no longer constipated

your friends as the next shot, a **zip pan** along the side of the five-a-side football pitch, introduces this new location (see Style: Cinematography). The next cut is to a shot of friends Renton, Sick Boy, Begbie, Spud and Tommy grouped in front of a goal.

A succinct example of functions served by the voice-over occurs during a **long shot** of Renton walking past a block of flats. This is early in the narrative, just after he has inserted opium suppositories into his backside. As he walks into the left-hand side of the shot, **non-diegetic music**, from Georges Bizet's 'Carmen', plays on the soundtrack. The voice-over explains how heroin makes him constipated, but that his last hit is fading away.

During this explanation, Renton walks towards the right-hand side of the shot. He stops, doubles up and groans that he is no longer constipated as he staggers out of shot. Voice-over enables narrative information to be quickly conveyed. The juxtaposition between classical music, Renton's physical contortions and the deadpan voice-over accentuates the comic urgency of the situation.

Renton's voice-over helps make *Trainspotting* accessible to a wide range of English-speaking audiences (see Contexts: Cultural Contexts: Representing Scotland). Ewan McGregor's delivery of the voice-over, in a light Scottish accent, maximises the narrative's intelligibility. His voice-over contrasts with the heavier Scottish accents some of the other actors, such as Ewen Bremner as Spud and Robert Carlyle as Begbie, use in their performances. Renton's voice-over interprets their actions and motivations for audiences who might not understand all of their dialogue. A joke is made of this process at the start of the Volcano club sequence. The voice-over temporarily stops and subtitles translate Tommy's and Spud's conversation.

UNRESTRICTED NARRATION

There is some use of unrestricted narration in *Trainspotting*. There are occasions in the narrative where the spectator sees and knows more than Renton could. Renton is not present during Spud's job interview on speed. This sequence establishes Spud as an amiable buffoon (see Character). Yet at the end of it, Renton's voice-over commends Spud's performance.

space for the spectator

A later sequence, without any voice-over, crosscuts between three couples having sex in different locations (see Style: Editing). Crosscutting shows the spectator more than Renton could see or know. Nevertheless, of the three male characters involved, the comparison favours Renton. Spud is comatose, and the realisation that the videotape of them having sex has been stolen proves to be a passion killer for both Tommy and Lizzy.

Narration becomes noticeably less restricted in *Trainspotting*'s closing sequence. Renton's journey through London with the bag of money he has just stolen from his friends is crosscut with shots of Begbie smashing up their hotel room after realising what has happened. Police arrive and Sick Boy and Spud slink away. The film's final image is of something else Renton could not see or know about. It is a shot, from inside a locker, of Spud picking up a wad of money Renton has left for him, smiling, and closing the locker door. Unrestricted narration in *Trainspotting*'s closing sequence maps out the final state of the relationships and parallelisms between characters within the narrative (see Character). It also opens up space for the spectator to reflect upon Renton's fate and the larger issues raised by the closing lines of his voice-over (see Opening/Close).

art cinema influences

In one interview, producer Andrew Macdonald cited *I Vitelloni* (Federico Fellini, 1953) as a film *Trainspotting* could be compared to. *I Vitelloni*'s episodic narrative is about the aimless lives of five friends in a provincial Italian town. One character leaves the others behind at the end of the film. *I Vitelloni* is a classic of art cinema. David Bordwell, in chapter ten of his book *Narration in the Fiction Film*, argues that art cinema narratives are episodic rather than tightly plotted in a conventional sense. Characters in this type of film have few clearly defined goals to achieve or deadlines to meet. They tend to drift aimlessly from one apparently random event to the next while crises build up which, sooner or later, they are forced to confront (see Character).

The high point of art cinema was the 1950s and 1960s when directors such as Fellini (Italy), Alain Resnais (France), Ingmar Bergman (Sweden) and Satyajit Ray (India) were at their most productive. In Britain, the high point came later. It was only in the 1980s that conditions within the British film industry enabled a diverse group of British films indebted to the traditions of art cinema to emerge (see Contexts: Industrial).

Trainspotting draws upon art cinema traditions, albeit in a highly selective way. It incorporates a certain number of art cinema's narrative devices but integrates them with other quite different influences. Art cinema often moves at a leisurely pace and, on first viewing, is sometimes difficult to comprehend or interpret. The influence of music video on *Trainspotting*'s narrative offsets these tendencies. The action moves at a dynamic pace and the film as a whole – and every sequence within it – is designed for immediate impact (see Little Hits Of Sensation).

character

EPISODIC NARRATION

David Bordwell (1985) discusses how episodic narration in art cinema constructs protagonists who 'slid[e] passively from one situation to another' because they have few clear objectives to achieve. This is most evident in the earlier part of *Trainspotting*, up to baby Dawn's death, but to a certain extent it persists throughout the narrative. Renton tends to drift and be reactive rather than proactive. He copes with, responds to or takes advantage of the various situations he finds himself in rather than actively causing events to happen (see Contexts: Ideology: Post-Thatcherism). For example, it is Diane who controls the outcome of their encounter at the Volcano club and Tommy who drags him, Sick Boy and Spud out to the countryside.

The drug deal near to the end of *Trainspotting*'s narrative gives Renton, Begbie, Sick Boy and Spud a specific goal to achieve, and moves the narrative to its conclusion. However, even this comes about by chance. The drug deal is not something any of the characters have been planning for or working towards throughout the narrative. The drugs become available due to the unexpected, unexplained appearance in a pub near the docks of two Russian sailors with a surprisingly large amount of heroin for sale. Plot in this sense is therefore not the most important factor in *Trainspotting*. What really drives the narrative and links its various episodes together is the development of its main characters, the growing tensions between them and the crisis in Renton's values.

PARALLELISM

Narration and voice-over in *Trainspotting* privilege Renton's attitudes (see Narration). His voice-over after taking the money from the drug deal comments on the other characters. He affirms contempt for Begbie – who he doesn't give a shit about – a cynical affinity with Sick Boy – who he says would have acted in the same way – and sympathy for Spud, who he says would never hurt anyone. (See Narration: Unrestricted Narration and Contexts: Cultural Contexts: New Lads.) This is preceded by a frank admission that he has ripped off his mates. The seeds of this outcome are sown in the extensive use of parallelism in the earlier part of the narrative.

Most film narratives rely upon a combination of two types of narrative logic; cause and effect relationships and parallelisms. Art cinema narration tends to emphasise parallelisms, for example similarities and differences between characters, rather than cause and effect relationships. One of the main purposes of *Trainspotting*'s opening sequence, for example, is to parallel different characters' attitudes towards drug use (see Contexts: Cultural Contexts: Drug Debates).

Parallelism and cause and effect relations can operate simultaneously. There is a strong cause and effect relationship between *Trainspotting*'s first and second sequence. Renton wakes from his stupor in Swanney's drug den at the end of the opening sequence and announces that he's off the skag. The effect of this is carried through to the next sequence where he prepares to go through the process of coming off heroin. In general, however, sequences in the earlier part of *Trainspotting*'s narrative are linked through parallelisms rather than cause and effect relationships. They focus on exploring similarities, differences and relationships between characters.

The sequence with Renton and Sick Boy in the park is not strongly

cynical and articulate

connected in cause and effect terms with the sequences preceding and following it. The main link between them is through parallelism of character traits and attitudes. Renton's voice-over makes this clear at the beginning of the sequence in the park. He says that his friends are so like himself that he doesn't like looking at them.

The sequence in the park establishes Sick Boy as being every bit as cynical and articulate as Renton. The next sequence establishes Spud's bumbling, amiable nature and the warm friendship between him and Renton. This differs from the competitive relationship between Renton and Sick Boy in the preceding sequence. Parallelism in the next sequence highlights pertinent differences between Renton, Begbie and Tommy. Begbie is established as the most violent character when he casually starts a fight in a pub. Tommy is established as the most naïve because he always tells the truth. Parallelism continues through editing after the characters have been to the Volcano club. Crosscutting highlights similarities and differences between three couples having sex in different locations (see Style: Editing).

THE BOUNDARY SITUATION

David Bordwell argues in *Narration in the Fiction Film* that the 'boundary situation' is often an important organising factor in art cinema narration. Rather than consisting of a series of unconnected episodes, art cinema narratives will be dominated by or gradually lead towards an existential crisis. This crisis raises questions about the meaning, purpose and direction of characters' lives. Very often these questions are not conclusively resolved (see Opening/Close). Nevertheless, the boundary situation gives shape and structure to the narrative.

This is relevant to the contrast in tone between the earlier and later parts of *Trainspotting*'s narrative. *Empire* reviewer Neil Jeffries noted a 'stunning turnaround' which begins after baby Dawn dies. Other negative consequences of heroin use follow in rapid succession: Renton, Sick Boy and Spud go on a shoplifting spree; Renton and Spud are caught and Spud gets a prison sentence; Renton overdoses and goes through the gruesome ordeal of coming off heroin; Tommy, who has just started using heroin, is diagnosed as HIV positive.

friendships within the group unravel

The overriding logic connecting the sequences here is not one of cause and effect. Dawn's death, Renton's overdose and Tommy's diagnosis are, on one level, arbitrary events caused by pure bad luck. The strongest connection between these sequences is that they form part of an intensifying boundary situation. Renton's voice-over, just before he and Spud are caught, reflects upon the inevitability of eventually reaching a crisis point, which he realises was bound to happen. After Spud has gone to prison and Begbie has hurled abuse at Spud's mother, Renton's voice-over elaborates on what these events mean for him as he explains how he wishes he had gone down instead of Spud, but instead he feels incredibly alone.

Friendships within the group unravel further after Begbie and Sick Boy follow Renton to London and as the drug deal proceeds.

Issues raised by the boundary situation become more prominent in the latter part of *Trainspotting*'s narrative and the comedy diminishes. When comedy does occur, it is darker. In the earlier part of the narrative, Renton's visit to the bookies' toilet has a slapstick quality, as does Spud's accident with the sheets at Gail's parents' house. After the narrative's 'stunning turnaround', the tone of the comedy changes. The hallucinations Renton experiences when locked in his bedroom are as harrowing as they are humorous. Begbie appears under his sheets threatening to kick the heroin out of his system and Renton sees game show host Dale Winton quizzing his parents about HIV on the television. In London, Begbie responds violently to Renton's joke about his encounter with a transsexual (see Contexts: Cultural Contexts: New Lads).

chronology

Chronology is fractured during the earlier part of *Trainspotting*'s narrative. The order and precise duration of the story (see **plot** and **story**), as well as the frequency and duration of certain events within it, is difficult to determine. This is quite common in art cinema narration. A famous example is *Last Year at Marienbad* (Alain Resnais, 1961), which takes chronological ambiguity to an extreme. *Trainspotting* does not take its play

the narrative is deliberately blurred

with chronology anywhere near to the disorientating extreme that *Last Year at Marienbad* does. Nevertheless, the earlier part of *Trainspotting* is deliberately blurred.

The main chronological ambiguity in the earlier part of *Trainspotting*'s narrative hinges around shoplifting in Princes Street. Shots of characters shoplifting from the opening 'Lust for Life' sequence recur in the sequence immediately after Dawn dies. Each shoplifting sequence also contains shots which are not contained in the other one. The second time shoplifting is represented in the plot, it is accompanied on the soundtrack by instrumental passages from the melancholy Blur track 'Sing' (see Style: Music). Whether the shoplifting occurs once or twice in the story is not entirely clear.

The recurrence of several shots from the opening 'Lust for Life' scene in the later 'Sing' shoplifting sequence might suggest that it is the same story incident. In this case, all narrative events between the two representations of the shoplifting spree in the plot would belong to an extended **flashback**. This flashback might begin after the last shoplifting shot in the opening 'Lust for Life' sequence. Renton stops in front of a car and the shot ends in a freeze frame with a title bearing his name superimposed upon it. The flashback would end when this shot is repeated at the end of the shoplifting sequence after Dawn's death. This time, instead of a freeze frame, the shot ends with a store detective crashing into Renton and a cut to the courtroom sequence. Everything from the five-a-side football match up to Dawn's death would therefore occur prior to one shoplifting spree in the story.

This is a plausible way of comprehending the earlier part of *Trainspotting*'s narrative, but the possibility that a flashback might not have occurred is equally plausible. The titled freeze frame shot of Renton forms part of a series of similar shots used to introduce all the main characters in the opening sequence. Renton's freeze frame could simply be part of this series rather than the beginning of a flashback. In the opening 'Lust for Life' sequence, there is no definite indication in the editing, music or voice-over that a flashback has begun. A cut is used to end the titled freeze frame shot of Renton, rather than for example a **dissolve** or **fade** which might more

fractured within individual sequences

obviously signal the beginning of a flashback. The music does not change and Renton's voice-over continues without giving any hint that a flashback has begun (see Narration: Voice-over).

In some films, the source of a character's voice-over and the beginning of a flashback is clearly located in a framing sequence. For example, Renton's voice-over can be contrasted with the more classical use of the protagonist's voice-over in the famous British film *Kind Hearts and Coronets* (Robert Hamer, 1949). In this film, the voice-over is motivated by framing sequences of the protagonist reading his memoirs at the beginning and end of the film. This enables the spectator to clearly understand the chronological order of events. Within *Kind Hearts and Coronets*, it is absolutely clear that the majority of the narrative is an extended flashback and that the events in the flashback occurred before the framing sequences. *Trainspotting*'s chronology is more indeterminate than this.

Chronology in the earlier part of *Trainspotting*'s narrative is also fractured within individual sequences. In the opening sequence, it is not possible to be certain about whether the five-a-side football match occurs before or after the drug taking at Swanney's. The final shot of Renton running away after shoplifting is followed by two shots of him at Swanney's drug den. These are followed by shots of the football match. The Calton Athletic players take a free kick, hitting Renton on the head with the football. Shots of him falling backwards are crosscut with shots of him falling backwards at Swanney's (see Style: Editing).

Renton cannot be in two places at the same time in *Trainspotting*'s opening sequence, so one event must have happened before the other. The chronological order of the football match and the events at Swanney's drug den is left unclear. This approach to chronology is partly related to the influence of music video on *Trainspotting*'s narrative (see Little Hits Of Sensation). In music videos, style and immediate visual impact is often more important than chronology.

In the sequence where Tommy tries heroin for the first time while Iggy Pop's 'Nightclubbing' is on the soundtrack, Renton is slumped in a chair. There is a cut to a shot of Sick Boy putting on a tie while talking about

consistent chronology no longer matters

Sean Connery and 1960s' Bond girls. This is followed by shots of Renton stealing money from his family and heroin being prepared. In a **shot/reverse shot** structure, Renton is slumped against a wall and Tommy explains how Lizzy has left him. Sick Boy continues with his monologue and getting dressed. Renton is again slumped semi-conscious in a chair. Then the shot/reverse shot structure involving Tommy and Renton slumped against a wall resumes as Tommy asks Renton for his first hit and hands him money to pay for it. In the next shot, Sick Boy continues talking and getting dressed.

In this sequence, framing, background detail, costume and character movement in the two shot/reverse shot structures involving Tommy and Renton are identical. Framing, background detail, costume and character movement are also identical in all three shots of Sick Boy. Consequently the precise order and frequency of events within this sequence is uncertain. The consistency of framing, background detail, costume and character movement in the shots implies that only one interaction between Renton and Sick Boy and one interaction between Renton and Tommy takes place. If these were different occasions, it would be more plausible for the characters to be in different positions on each occasion. Yet if there is only one interaction between Renton and Sick Boy and one interaction between Renton and Tommy in this sequence, there is no way of knowing which takes place first.

The overarching effect of the chronological ambiguities in the earlier part of *Trainspotting*'s narrative is to underline that this is an aimless lifestyle where consistent chronology no longer matters (see Character: Episodic Narration). When the narrative reaches its boundary situation, this changes. At this point, Renton's experience of the lifestyle represented in the earlier part of the narrative moves towards crisis point. Whatever order previous events occurred in, and however many times they occurred, the narrative now takes a different turn. Previously, distinctions between past and present have become blurred. The boundary situation forces Renton to face the future, whatever it holds (see Character: The Boundary Situation). His voice-over predicts after Dawn dies that things were going to be even worse than they already were.

space

Immediately after they visit the Scottish countryside, Renton, Sick Boy and Spud return to using heroin. Renton is appalled by Tommy's enthusiasm for this supposedly pure Scottish space (see Contexts: Cultural Contexts: Representing Scotland). Later in the narrative, Renton's move to London is to a certain extent a significant development. It seems to offer a possible way out of the boundary situation he finds himself in. Yet whether London is the solution is open to question. In many respects it offers more of the same rather than something different and better.

London resembles Edinburgh in *Trainspotting*. The narrative primarily unfolds within interior spaces in both locations (see Style: Production Design). Sequences representing Renton's everyday routine in both locations also resemble each other. Renton's work as a London estate agent is shown in a sequence which crosscuts between his office and him showing a property to clients. His voice-over describes his new job in terms which compare it to criminal activity, describing profit and loss, subletting and dividing, cheating and scamming.

Earlier in the narrative, the 'Nightclubbing' sequence in Edinburgh represents Renton and other characters stealing to feed their habit. Heroin addiction is represented as hard work. Renton's voice-over explains that it is a full-time business.

Differences between Edinburgh and London and Renton's lifestyle in both places are also minimised by the way he moves between them. A **montage sequence** of clichéd images of London life magically transports Renton from an underclass life in Edinburgh to an enterprising one in London (see Contexts: Genre: Swinging London Cycle). The indefinite **ellipsis** in *Trainspotting*'s narrative created by this montage sequence sustains the impression of Renton as a protagonist who drifts rather than one who has clearly defined objectives (see Character: Episodic Narration). The actual process of him seeking a job as an estate agent is not represented. Renton does not talk explicitly about a change of values until the closing lines of his voice-over at the very end of the narrative.

opening/close

In *Trainspotting*'s opening sequence, Renton's voice-over angrily lists and rejects a series of consumer items and the conventional lifestyle associated with them.

The voice-over's closing lines at the end of the narrative invert the opening, proclaiming he's going to embrace those very consumer items he had earlier rejected.

At the end of *Trainspotting*'s narrative, after finally leaving his friends behind, Renton claims to be ready to clean up and move on. Renton's voice-over apparently embraces consumerism, but what could be a tone of mock enthusiasm in his voice suggests a lack of conviction. Moreover, as Sarah Street points out in her essay on *Trainspotting*, the film sometimes juxtaposes different elements to generate a complex range of meanings. The juxtaposition of voice-over and image within the closing sequence places a question mark over *Trainspotting*'s conclusion.

In the final shot of Renton in the film, he walks towards the camera, moving into **extreme close-up**. His smiling face begins to blur, eventually disappearing into nothingness. This image of oblivion and his voice-over's final words, which say he's looking ahead to the day he dies, link his decision to 'choose life' with death. The implication is that consumerism and the conventional lifestyle associated with it is a lifeless dead end. This is what Renton's voice-over asserted at the beginning of the narrative.

A final narrative device *Trainspotting* derives from art cinema narration is its ambiguous ending (see Art Cinema Influences). Renton has been through a boundary situation but it is difficult to be certain about whether or not this has transformed him as a character (see Character: The Boundary Situation). Has he really discovered new values to believe in and found a new sense of direction, or are the final lines of his voice-over the supreme example of his profound cynicism and opportunism? Regardless of whether he is sincere or cynical, does the narration at this point consign him to oblivion?

The end of *Trainspotting*'s narrative can be understood as implying that Renton is going nowhere and there is no possibility of choosing a viable, meaningful future. This would be consistent with the lack of direction which has characterised his actions throughout much of the narrative (see Character: Episodic Narration). Perhaps a positive choice is impossible and to choose life or not to choose life are equally futile options.

Unrestricted narration at the end of *Trainspotting* encourages the spectator to reflect upon Renton's fate and the larger issues it raises (see Narration: Unrestricted Narration). Renton's walk towards the camera and the phrasing of his voice-over directly addresses the spectator, saying he's going to be just like us. Renton does not escape from consumerism, however much he might have wanted to or might still want to. The use of direct address confronts the spectator with the suggestion that he or she may not have any more of a real choice in this matter than Renton has. This ambiguous critical awareness/acceptance of consumerism extended to *Trainspotting*'s marketing which played with similar ideas (see Contexts: Marketing).

style

Style is palpable throughout *Trainspotting*. The soundtrack and the costume design incorporate diverse elements from the history of popular music and youth subcultural style. The film's production design constructs a visually arresting environment for the narrative to unfold within. Cinematography and editing employ many *outré* techniques. Harlan Kennedy (1996) points out that the film runs through 'a gleeful repertoire of frozen frames, card-shuffling montage sequences, queasy false perspectives, and fantastical visual punctuation'. *Trainspotting*'s style is uncompromisingly energetic and can be enjoyed for its own sake. At the same time, it is possible to discern narrative and thematic justifications or, as Danny Boyle put it, 'organic reasons' for particular stylistic choices (see Contexts: Critical Responses).

music

Trainspotting represents popular music as being in a constant state of flux. When Renton and Begbie visit a club in London the music played there is quite different from the 1980s' hits 'Temptation' and 'Atomic' played in the Volcano club back in Scotland when Renton first meets Diane. As early 1990s' dance music plays in the London club, Renton's voice-over muses how the world, music and drugs are all changing. This acceptance of diversity is the only comment made about music in Renton's voice-over. It never comments upon specific pieces of **diegetic** or **non-diegetic music**. Value judgements and characters' expressions of preference for particular types of music are kept to a minimum and are always open to question.

The only musicians directly referred to within *Trainspotting*'s diegesis are Lou Reed and Iggy Pop. They enjoy a special status within the film because both have been associated with heroin. In the park, Renton and Sick Boy debate the value of Lou Reed's music. In the Volcano club, Tommy tells Spud he has bought tickets for Iggy Pop's concert on the night of Lizzy's birthday. Lizzy, presumably not a fan, has told Tommy he must choose between her and Iggy. Smoking hash together just before the narrative shifts to London, Diane feeds Renton the lines his voice-over later repeats in the London club about the world, music and drugs all changing. Conflating David Bowie's Ziggy Stardust persona with Iggy Pop, Diane tells Renton it is time to stop dreaming about heroin and Ziggy Pop and move on.

Lou Reed and Iggy Pop are legendary figures within the history of popular music, but whenever one character in *Trainspotting* asserts their importance, another one denies it. Renton corrects Diane, telling her it is Iggy not Ziggy Pop. Her only response is a bored 'whatever'. If popular music is in a constant state of flux, then even the status of these legendary figures must be open to question. As far as music is concerned, *Trainspotting* takes nothing for granted because the film is designed to encompass and appeal to a wide spectrum of youth audience tastes and likes.

'Youth' and youthful tastes in music are difficult to define and represent in film. When does youth begin and when does it end: at thirteen or eighteen; at twenty-four or thirty-four? What type of music should be associated with contemporary youth? These issues are taken up in Karen Lury's essay 'Here and Then: Space, Place and Nostalgia in British Youth Cinema of the 1990s'. She compares *Trainspotting* to earlier examples of British youth films to demonstrate how, if a film targeted at youth audiences defines contemporary youth too narrowly, it can easily alienate part of its potential audience.

Lury argues that *Trainspotting* gained a considerable edge over other 1990s' British youth films such as *Shopping* (Paul Anderson, 1993) and *Blue Juice* (Carl Prechnezer, 1995). These films are set in the present and establish clear distinctions between authentic and inauthentic types of music. *Shopping* tries to be as up to date as possible in its selection of music. In this film, cassettes of uncool 1980s' music are thrown one by one out of the window of a stolen car. In *Blue Juice*, a London-based record producer is made to realise that he has drained the soul out of original recordings he has been sampling. Both films are less inclusive in their use of music than *Trainspotting*.

Trainspotting does not advocate any particular type of music as better than another. It includes an eclectic selection of music on its soundtrack. If trends change and musical taste is always diverse, then it is best not to associate films or characters within them too closely with any particular type of music. The wide spectrum of music in *Trainspotting* is primarily non-diegetic. This enables it to comment on characters and narrative events without necessarily defining the characters as fans of any particular kind of music.

The primarily non-diegetic music in *Trainspotting* ranges across a broad spectrum of 1990s' music as well as music from previous decades. Dance music and Britpop, both important musical genres of the 1990s, are well represented. Leftfield, Underworld, Blur and Pulp contribute songs to the soundtrack. The inclusion of classic tracks such as Iggy Pop's 'Lust for Life', Lou Reed's 'Perfect Day' and a version of Blondie's 'Atomic' broadens the soundtrack's musical range beyond the contemporary.

There is a shift from older to more recent music on the soundtrack as *Trainspotting*'s narrative unfolds. This contributes to the impression that the historical period covered by the narrative is from the 1980s to the early 1990s. However, the most crucial function of *Trainspotting*'s eclectic selection of music is that it allows diverse audiences to enjoy the soundtrack without feeling the film is offering a narrow representation of contemporary youth which excludes them.

Non-diegetic music on *Trainspotting*'s soundtrack plays a vital role in audiences' understanding and enjoyment of the film. It comments upon, adds nuances to and enhances the narrative's emotional resonance. 'Lust for Life', the classic late 1970s' track played in the opening 'Choose Life' sequence invokes Iggy Pop's status as a drugs and music icon who returned from drug addiction to continue making great music. It asserts a will to live and clean up as well as celebrating the pleasures and degradations of drug use. It augments the film's representation of heroin users as more than simply victims or products of their social circumstances (see Narrative & Form: Narration: Restricted Narration and Contexts: Cultural Contexts: Drug Debates and Genre).

The mournful 1990s' Blur track 'Sing' is later played over some of the same shots featured in the opening sequence (see Narrative & Form: Chronology). Here the music accentuates the devastating numbness the characters feel after Dawn's death (see Narrative & Form: Character: The Boundary Situation). The different meanings and emotions 'Lust for Life' and 'Sing' contribute to visually similar sequences demonstrate how important a factor music is for generating emotion and meaning in the film.

Music in *Trainspotting* adds meaning and significance to the film, and the film in turn added new meaning and significance to the music. In *Trainspotting*, 'Perfect Day', with its chorus of: 'You're going to reap just what you sow', adds poignancy to images of Renton's overdose. It epitomises the film's stance on drug taking (see Contexts: Cultural Contexts: Drug Debates). Renton reaps both pleasure and pain as this soothing piece of music plays on the soundtrack over images of him close to death.

After the release of the film and its soundtrack albums, an advertisement for the BBC was screened repeatedly on BBC television. An eclectic range of musicians sang sections of 'Perfect Day'. They included older figures such as David Bowie and younger ones such as Boyzone. They represented a range of musical styles and traditions, from the opera singer Lesley Garratt to Lou Reed himself.

The technique of employing such a wide range of singers with such a wide range of styles in the BBC advertisement is very similar to *Trainspotting*'s broadening of its potential audience appeal through a diverse mixture of old and new music. This diversity emphasised that the BBC caters to wide audiences. The choice of 'Perfect Day', a classic song associated with a recent trend-setting film, emphasised that the BBC combines the classic and the modern. This advertisement provides one example of how *Trainspotting* became more than just a successful film. The *Trainspotting* phenomenon has become a cultural reference point.

'essential wear for nutters'

Aspects of it have been recycled for use in various other contexts (see Contexts: Filmography).

fashion

Fashion in *Trainspotting* is as subtly inclusive and non-specific as music. Each central male character is associated with a distinctive style of dress. Renton, Sick Boy and Spud are differentiated, to a certain extent, from the straighter characters and marked out as representatives of fashionable youth. Their styles of dress are not, however, too closely identified with any particular youth subculture, but instead combine elements drawn from several different ones.

Sick Boy is the most obviously, perhaps excessively style-conscious character. He often wears sharp suits and always sports bleached hair. Renton's appearance draws together diverse elements of youth style in a less obvious way. This is appropriate to his narrative role as the character who spends most time on screen (see Narrative & Form: Narration: Restricted Narration). In visual terms, he has to be the most broadly acceptable character, epitomising youth style without alienating sections of the audience. Renton's favoured outfit is a T-shirt, jacket or top, tight jeans, trainers, cropped hair and earring in his left ear. Spud's style is somewhere between Sick Boy's and Renton's. Collectively these characters display a range of male youth styles for various audiences to enjoy.

Tommy is always dressed more conventionally than Sick Boy, Renton and Spud, and his haircut is unremarkable. In visual terms, this sets him apart from them. His comparatively neutral appearance reinforces his role as an innocent character (see Narrative & Form: Character: Parallelism). Begbie is also dressed more conventionally than the other central male characters, but in his case this is pushed to an extreme. Begbie sports an unfashionable moustache, longish, often slicked-back hair and, in Robert Carlyle's words, 'white socks ... essential wear for nutters' (*The Face*, February 1996). Throughout the narrative, he wears an array of casual rather than subcultural clothes as well as a gold neck chain, wrist chain and rings on both hands. His left hand carries a tattoo of his name. The conventionality of his appearance is exaggerated to a point where, combined with his increasingly violent actions, it becomes menacing (see Contexts: Cultural Contexts: New Lads).

Tommy and Begbie are fixed into certain roles within *Trainspotting*'s narrative by their straight appearance. One of the reasons why Renton survives the ups and downs of the narrative is because of his pragmatism and flexibility (see Contexts: Ideology: Post-Thatcherism). He adapts his personal style for different contexts. He wears a suit before his and Spud's job interviews, when he goes to court, and when he works as a London estate agent. Renton comes close to embodying the principle of stylistic diversity which underlies *Trainspotting*'s use of music.

Diane is the only character who adheres to this principle even more effectively than Renton. There is no discrepancy for her between wearing a sparkling blue dress at the Volcano club in the evening and a schoolgirl's uniform during the day. Diane is the person who feeds Renton the line about the world, music and drugs changing which precipitates his decision to go to London (see Music).

To a certain extent, Diane can be seen as a powerful female character who refuses, through fashion, fixed notions of who she should be. On the other hand it can be argued that she is not a particularly important narrative agent in her own right. She picks Renton up in the Volcano club and insists he continue to see her afterwards, but does little else within the narrative apart from relay information, via letter, about what his male friends are doing after he has gone to London. Diane is defined within *Trainspotting*'s narrative almost exclusively in terms of her relationship with Renton and she is marked out as a spectacle to be looked at by men (see Contexts: Cultural Contexts: New Lads). Each time she appears, as clubber and schoolgirl, she is initially seen through a **point-of-view shot** from Renton's perspective.

production design

Realist films such as *Raining Stones* (Ken Loach, 1993) tend to be shot in exterior and interior locations where the working- or lower middle-class characters these films typically represent would actually live. *Trainspotting*

production design

seductive and repulsive elements

is quite different. With a few significant exceptions, much of the film is shot in a series of interiors (see Contexts: Cultural Contexts: Representing Scotland). This is as true of the sections of the narrative located in London as it is of those in Edinburgh (see Narrative & Form: Space). The main difference between these cities, underlined by shots of characters sleeping head to toe in Renton's flat and their hotel room, is that there is less living space available in London. This heightens tensions between them.

Swanney's drug den, where most of the drug taking in the earlier part of *Trainspotting*'s narrative occurs, is the film's most elaborate set. Different parts of it are coloured in visually arresting shades of green, yellow, red and blue. Walls are bare and some of them are knocked through to open up space. Furnishing is minimal, for example mattresses rather than beds. Floors are cluttered with bric-a-brac and semi-conscious people. In the latter part of the narrative, Renton's flat gradually begins to resemble Swanney's drug den. It becomes increasingly bare of furnishing and full of junk after Begbie and Sick Boy arrive. Less emphasis upon bold colours contributes to the more sombre tone of the latter part of the narrative (see Narrative & Form: Character: The Boundary Situation). One example is Tommy's drab, gloomy room in the last sequence he appears in before he dies.

Trainspotting's production design combines appealing colours with repulsive elements such as an appallingly dirty toilet and a replica dead baby. This combination of seductive and repulsive elements emphasises the pleasures as well as the negative aspects of the characters' lifestyle.

In certain shots, particularly within the earlier part of the narrative, production design adds visual lustre to the characters and their situation. One example is the **tracking shot** in the opening sequence which moves along a corridor. It travels past a room containing baby Dawn to enter another room where Sick Boy, Allison, Spud and Swanney are shooting up. A semi-demolished wall behind them opens onto yet another room. In addition to revealing various areas within the den, a spectrum of eye-catching colours is encompassed within this shot. Other shots flatten space, giving the film the vividness and abstractness of a simple comic strip style. The next shot is of Swanney crouching in the foreground next to a chair. The uniform red of the kitchen area behind him contrasts with his black leather waistcoat, bathing the top part of the shot in colour and compressing background space.

Trainspotting departs from the realist style one might expect from a British film dealing with this subject matter (see Background: Reading *Trainspotting*). What moves *Trainspotting*'s style beyond straightforward realism is its distorted spatial dimensions, heightened colour scheme and flights of fancy which partially or momentarily transform a degraded environment into a richer experience for characters and audiences alike.

Renton's visit to the bookies' toilet exemplifies *Trainspotting*'s transformation of degraded environments. He dashes across a urine-soaked floor into a tiny shit-streaked cubicle with a clogged toilet bowl and a chain that breaks. He squats down to relieve himself, then realises the opium suppositories inserted into his backside have dropped into the bowl. He fishes around in the bowl and gradually slides down to submerge into a calm blue underwater paradise. Brian Eno's calming 'Deep Blue Day' accompanies this action on the soundtrack. The music bridges both spaces as he emerges back up from the bowl into the filthy cubicle. This is an extreme example of how sensual and squalid elements are intertwined in *Trainspotting*'s visual design.

cinematography

Trainspotting's cinematography can be contrasted with the type of cinematography employed in British realist films, for example by cinematographers such as Chris Menges or Barry Ackroyd working with directors such as Ken Loach (see Background: Reading *Trainspotting*). There are different approaches to realist film making but, generally speaking, cinematography in this tradition tends to avoid striking effects of the kind employed in *Trainspotting*. Realist cinematography is sometimes recognised and praised as a specific style which, although it does not draw attention to itself, requires considerable expertise to achieve. It aims to make a film's representation of its subject matter seem convincingly grounded in an objective social reality.

cinematography style

radically detached from society

British realist cinematography often employs **soft lighting**, approximating natural lighting conditions, rather than dramatically highlighting particular characters in ways which set them apart from other characters. Unobtrusive camera positions, involving conventional **camera height** and **straight-on angle shots** focus attention on what is being represented in the shot rather than the cinematography itself. **Medium** and **long shots** are used to situate characters within their social environment. **Panning** and tracking, sometimes with a handheld camera, are usually motivated by apparently unanticipated character movements. This reinforces the impression for the **spectator** of **off-screen space** and the existence of a social world beyond the film which the cinematography is simply observing. The artistry of the cinematography in this tradition is subtle rather than overt.

Trainspotting's cinematography is not concerned with representing the social world and social interaction in the way a British realist film set on location would be. Exterior shots visualise Renton's voice-over comment that there is no such thing as society (see Contexts: Ideology: Post-Thatcherism). When Renton shoots an air rifle at a skinhead's dog early in the narrative, other people in the park are seen from Renton's and Sick Boy's perspective. Renton's and Sick Boy's point-of-view shots are partly **masked** to emphasise that they are looking through binoculars and the rifle's telescopic sight. This is a comedy sequence which also makes the point that Renton and Sick Boy are radically detached from the rest of society. Everyone else in the park is represented as a potential enemy.

Trainspotting's long and **extreme long shots** are usually devoid of passers-by or other social activities taking place in the background. Examples include Diane and Renton as the only people outside the Volcano club, Swanney waiting as a solitary figure in the middle of a housing estate for a taxi to dump Renton's overdosed body into and a lone figure, presumably Renton, walking across a London bridge after he has absconded with the proceeds of the drug deal. The shot of the London bridge is followed by the last shot of Renton in the film as he walks towards the camera (see Narrative & Form: Opening/Close). This last shot is held in **shallow focus**. This obscures passers-by and other background details. A realist style of cinematography would place more emphasis on filling in this detail, representing a social context characters belong to and which their actions could be typical of.

Trainspotting's cinematography is distinguished by an inventiveness and a striving for effect which brands the film as markedly different, in stylistic terms, from most other British films of the 1980s and early 1990s. Various aspects of the cinematography display this. The shot of Renton, Sick Boy, Begbie, Spud and Tommy grouped in front of a goal in the film's opening sequence highlights the cinematography's overtly stylised rather than self-effacing nature. The characters pose for the camera, rather than pretending it is not there as they would in a realist film.

Lighting in *Trainspotting* is often organised to construct dramatic effects rather than to resemble natural lighting as is the case with more strictly realist styles of cinematography. One example is the long shadows across the ceiling and walls in the sequence where Renton, Sick Boy, Begbie and Spud first discuss the drug deal. This was modelled on a sequence in the famous, stylistically adventurous film noir *Touch of Evil* (Orson Welles, 1958). Lighting also augments the colours in Swanney's drug den.

Trainspotting's cinematography employs a wide spectrum of techniques involving the movement and position of the camera and the use of different lenses to stretch or reduce space. A **short-focal length** 10mm lens produces a tunnel effect, lengthening and narrowing Renton's bedroom when his parents lock him in to come off heroin and he starts to hallucinate. Tracking movements make the bed and room appear to slide around. Camera angles maximise horrific images. In an extreme **low angle shot** a dead baby falls down from the ceiling. The baby's fall is picked up by a rapid downwards camera movement in the next shot, a **high angle close-up** of Renton's screaming face.

The brash cinematography in *Trainspotting* can be related to narrative or thematic functions as well as being enjoyed as an exercise in style for its own sake. The short-focal length lens which stretches space during Spud's job interview can be related to the speed he has just taken. A tracking shot along a corridor in Swanney's den moves urgently towards Allison as she emerges from a room screaming after realising Dawn is dead. A

playful and innovative

subsequent camera movement creeps slowly around the edge of Dawn's cot, hesitating to reveal her death to the spectator and the other characters. Shots from **impossible camera positions**, such as from inside the chamber of a heroin needle, are first and foremost striking images but they can also have narrative or thematic significance as well. In this case they show impure residue from the hit which causes Renton to overdose at Swanney's.

Camera height is important in *Trainspotting*. The camera tracks along Renton's prone body the first time he falls over from taking heroin. This low height continues in the next shot revealing various areas of Swanney's den (see Style: Production Design). What explains many shots taken from a similarly low height, according to the production team, is the fact that junkies spend a considerable amount of time flat out on the floor. The use of a low camera height in many shots is consistent with the production team's intention to represent the subjective experience of heroin users rather than to take a more distanced view of them as victims or products of their social circumstances (see Narrative & Form: Narration: Restricted Narration and Contexts: Cultural Contexts: Drug Debates and Genre).

This strategy of positioning the camera at a similar height to *Trainspotting*'s often supine characters is taken to a logical extreme when Renton overdoses at Swanney's. As the heroin takes effect, Renton sinks into the floor. Several bizarre, extreme low angle point-of-view shots looking up from beneath the carpet follow. These continue during his journey to and inside the hospital. Some commentators have suggested that, since Renton is near death, these shots resemble the view from inside a coffin or literally represent the abject depths he has sunk to.

Cinematography in *Trainspotting* is constantly playful and innovative. The film contains numerous unusual, eye-catching shots which mark it out as a new departure in 1990s' British cinema. In some cases, the playfulness of these shots contribute to the film's comedy and its emphasis upon the pleasure as well as the grimness of the characters' lifestyle. In others, striking shots serve narrative or thematic functions. Playful cinematography was one of the stylistic elements audiences derived pleasure from and some critics attempted to interpret (see

abrupt transitions abound

Contexts: Critical Responses and Audience). The distinctive quality of its cinematography contributed to *Trainspotting*'s status as a landmark film within British film history (see Contexts: Filmography).

editing

The total number of shots in *Trainspotting* is higher than average for a film of this length. As with the cinematography, editing in *Trainspotting* often tends to be overt rather than subtle, drawing attention to itself as a stylistic element. Cuts rather than optical effects such as dissolves or fades are used to link sequences or move characters from one location to the next. For example, there is a cut from the shot of Renton emerging back up from the bowl in the bookies' toilet to a shot from a low height of his feet coming through a door as he enters his room. Renton's pulling himself fully out of the toilet bowl, his departure from the bookies and his journey home are not shown.

Similar examples of abrupt transitions between sequences and locations abound throughout *Trainspotting*. Renton decides to have another hit after Spud has been sent to prison. There is a cut from a low angle long shot of Renton leaping off a wall to a shot of him landing at Swanney's drug den and crouching on the floor preparing for his hit. Other ways of linking these shots would have produced different effects. A dissolve would have created a smoother transition between the two locations. A fade could have provided a moment for reflection, perhaps encouraging the spectator to think about the implications of Renton's decision to have another hit. The choice of a cut adds impact to Renton's movements while instantly crossing the thin line between being on and off heroin in this film.

Rapid cutting adds visceral impact to some otherwise banal sequences in *Trainspotting*. The sequence early in the narrative where Renton and Spud sit at a table sharing a milkshake prior to Spud's job interview is very rapidly edited. The first six shots in this sequence are held on screen for less than half a second each. In the first shot, from a straight-on angle shot at the side of the table, both Renton and Spud drink through straws from

editing

Trainspotting varies its editing rhythms

a milkshake in the centre of the frame. This is followed by individual low angle **medium close-ups** of each of them. The fourth shot is similar to the first, with the addition of a tracking movement back from the table. Two more low angle medium close-ups of Renton and Spud follow, held on screen for even less time than the previous two. The seventh shot, again from the side of the table, is held for much longer as the tracking movement continues.

Editing follows a pattern of repetition and variation in these first seven shots. Rapid editing and camera movement work together to add excitement to the banal situation of two characters quickly drinking a milkshake. Framing is also unusual. In Renton's medium close-ups, most of his face is excluded from the frame. The sequence continues with a rapidly edited **shot/reverse shot** structure. Spud talks about his pre-interview nerves. Renton gives him some speed. Spud's interview begins with an even more audacious editing pattern than the one used when he and Renton drink the milkshake. At the start of the interview, Spud sits in a chair rambling incoherently. **Jump cuts** between shots taken at different distances but from the same straight-on angle make him seem to instantaneously jump back and forth, closer to and then further away from the camera.

Trainspotting is full of playful editing experiments. As with the cinematography, these often serve narrative or thematic functions as well as being exercises in style for its own sake. Editing often works with the rhythm and tempo of actors' performances. Frantic editing just before and during Spud's interview takes its cue from Ewen Bremner's manic performance. The editing here responds to the way he fidgets, delivers his dialogue very quickly and uses his whole body to express nervousness and excitability. Renton and Sick Boy's escapade with the air rifle in the park, which precedes this sequence, is edited more slowly. This matches the calmer tone of the performances at this point. Although often rapidly edited, *Trainspotting* varies its editing rhythms from sequence to sequence according to what is being represented.

Editing experiments are balanced within *Trainspotting* by music, voice-over and other aspects of the editing. These prevent the editing style from becoming too fragmented or difficult to relate to. Renton's voice-over before he leaps off the wall explains that he needs to go to Swanney's drug den. This prevents the abrupt jump between locations from disorientating the spectator. Where necessary, the voice-over does the work of clarifying the narrative. This allows scope for experimental editing (see Narrative & Form: Narration: Voice-over). At the same time, the editing also uses conventional devices for ensuring narrative clarity and spatial continuity. *Trainspotting* often uses **eyeline matches** and **matches on action** as well as shot/reverse-shot structures for conversations between characters.

Anchored by the clarity and continuity that voice-over, music and conventional editing devices provide, *Trainspotting* is able to utilise a wide range of editing techniques. **Freeze frames** are used on several occasions. Sometimes an action begun by a character in one location is matched and completed in a different location, as when Renton leaps off the wall into Swanney's drug den. Sometimes an action by one character is paralleled by another in the following shot. During the 'Nightclubbing' sequence, shots of Renton, Tommy and Sick Boy falling on the floor follow each other in quick succession.

Editing in *Trainspotting* often plays on graphic contrasts rather than **graphic matches** between shots. In the opening sequence, Sick Boy talks to Allison in Swanney's den. The uniform red of the kitchen area behind Sick Boy in medium close-up contrasts with the clear bright light coming through the window in the next shot of Sick Boy facing Allison. Camera angles can also contrast dramatically from shot to shot. A straight-on close-up of Renton in the bookies' toilet is followed by another shot from an **impossible camera position** (see Cinematography). This is an extreme low angle shot from inside the toilet bowl as Renton peers down after realising his opium suppositories have dropped into it.

Trainspotting employs extensive **crosscutting**. This editing technique contributes to the film's dynamic style by rapidly linking diverse shots. Crosscutting also enables comparisons and contrasts between different experiences to be established. The first example is the football hitting Renton's head during the five-a-side match in the opening sequence. This

Archie Gemmill scored

is compared to the impact of a heroin hit in the next shot of Renton falling backwards in Swanney's drug den.

Similarities and differences between characters and ideas are also compared and contrasted through crosscutting. Diane and Renton having sex is crosscut with Lizzy and Tommy's and Gail and Spud's less successful encounters. A shot of Renton comparing sex with Archie Gemmill's goal against Holland is crosscut with a video image of the goal on Lizzy and Tommy's television (see Contexts: Cultural Contexts: New Lads). Editing in *Trainspotting* also makes more subtle comparisons. During the 'Nightclubbing' sequence, a shot of Renton receiving drugs from Swanney is followed by a shot of Renton in a doctor's surgery. Renton's voice-over explains how the National Health Service was the source of much of their drugs. Legal and illegal drugs and Swanney's and the doctor's social roles are implicitly compared (see Contexts: Cultural Contexts: Drug Debates).

contexts

industrial

Three industrial factors to consider when analysing a film are production, exhibition and distribution. In *Trainspotting*'s case this involves relating it to:

■ Developments in Channel 4's approach to film production in the 1990s

■ The growth of multiplex cinemas as a place to see films

■ The distribution practices of Polygram in Britain and Miramax in the USA

Channel 4 gave vital support for British film production during the 1980s and 1990s. Channel 4 provided all of *Trainspotting*'s £1.7 million production budget. This television channel was founded in 1982 to cater for audience tastes and minority groups not already served by British television and it encouraged innovative programme making. Rather than produce its own programmes, Channel 4 commissioned or bought them from independent production companies. It also became the first British television company to invest consistently in film production.

Through its *Film on Four* series, money went into independently produced films which would be screened on Channel 4, usually after a limited art house cinema release. Despite a politically conservative climate, many aesthetically and politically challenging low budget British feature films of the 1980s and early 1990s were partly or wholly financed by Channel 4 (see Ideology: Post-Thatcherism). These included films directed by Stephen Frears, Peter Greenaway, Derek Jarman, Terence Davies, Isaac Julien, Mike Leigh, Neil Jordan, Ken Loach, Sally Potter and Bill Douglas. This period is seen as the one when art cinema emerged in Britain (see Narrative & Form: Art Cinema Influences).

Channel 4 was initially funded through an arrangement which allowed it

significant crossover potential

a certain amount of freedom to experiment and innovate. Established ITV companies were responsible for selling Channel 4's advertising time in addition to their own, and paying the new channel a percentage of the income generated from the total advertising time sold. In its early years, Channel 4 was therefore shielded, up to a point, from commercial pressures. It did not always have to prioritise high audience ratings and selling advertising time over all other considerations. Its initial funding situation gave it the opportunity to develop and introduce to British audiences new types of television and film programming.

As the 1990s progressed, this situation changed. Channel 4 continued to build upon its reputation for funding adventurous film making, but after 1993 it became responsible for selling its own advertising. This placed it in a directly competitive relationship with other commercial television channels. With the advent of Channel 5, satellite and cable television there was more competition in the 1990s than in previous decades. A trend towards commissioning television programmes and feature films more likely to attract larger audiences and higher advertising revenues was noticeable on Channel 4 in the 1990s.

Trainspotting formed part of this trend. It was a particularly attractive prospect for Channel 4 in the mid-1990s because of the resounding critical and commercial success enjoyed by the *Trainspotting* team's first feature film, *Shallow Grave* (1994). Partly financed by Channel 4, and aided by an effective marketing campaign, *Shallow Grave* demonstrated the team's ability to deliver a film with significant crossover potential. In other words, it was successfully screened in art house cinemas and, much more crucial to its commercial success, multiplexes.

The first multiplex cinema opened in Britain in 1985. Well over a hundred had been built by the mid-1990s. In 1996, when *Trainspotting* was released, nearly half the total number of British cinema screens were located within multiplexes. As well as ensuring profitability, a good multiplex release also raises a film's profile. This is likely to boost sales and rentals when a film is later released on video and DVD. It also helps to attract high audience ratings and advertising revenues when it is shown on television. *Trainspotting* did all of these things.

production history

The proliferation of multiplexes in Britain contributed to a revival in cinema attendance. Cinema audience figures reached an all-time low in the early 1980s. After the advent of the multiplex, the total number of people going to the cinema each year increased steadily throughout the late 1980s and well into the late 1990s. Independent art house cinemas found it difficult to compete with the new multiplex chains. Audience figures in the art house sector did not rise significantly during this period.

Another issue is the enormous power of the major American distribution companies who handle Hollywood blockbusters and mainstream films. British multiplex screens tend to be dominated by these films. The film programming policies of the different multiplex cinema chains are very similar. At any one time, the same blockbusters and mainstream Hollywood films are likely to be exhibited in all the different multiplex chains. Depending upon demand, these films may be shown on several screens within a multiplex and retained for a month or more. This reduces the diversity of films on offer.

Some films which could not be described as either blockbusters or as entirely mainstream were widely seen in the 1990s, however. In this decade, two companies, Polygram in Britain and Miramax in America, emerged as important distributors of selected lower budget feature films (see Genre). Polygram was able to spend large sums of money marketing lower budget feature films deemed to have crossover potential. This is because it was, until 1998, 75% owned by the big Dutch electronics corporation, Philips. Like the major American distribution companies, Polygram could therefore draw upon substantial financial reserves to promote its films. Polygram's first outstanding success was *Four Weddings and a Funeral* (Mike Newell, 1994). Its next was *Trainspotting*, which took over £12 million at the British box office.

production history

After *Shallow Grave*'s success, producer Andrew Macdonald, director Danny Boyle and writer John Hodge could have moved into bigger budget film making, but they decided to continue working at a similar level for their next project, *Trainspotting*. Through *Shallow Grave* they had

a larger than life quality

established a good working relationship with David Aukin, Channel 4's head of drama. In early 1995, Aukin confirmed Channel 4 would provide 100% of *Trainspotting*'s production budget. He clearly believed the makers of *Shallow Grave* would produce another innovative film and secure a good return on Channel 4's investment. Polygram acquired *Trainspotting*'s UK distribution rights and allocated it an £850,000 marketing budget. This was much higher than the average amount spent promoting low budget British films.

Film production is an uncertain business and there was no way anyone could have predicted the extent of *Trainspotting*'s success. Yet producer Andrew Macdonald and director Danny Boyle were determined from the outset that their film should contain elements which appealed as widely as possible. Macdonald commented that he wanted *Trainspotting* to reach beyond the limited art house cinema circuit by attracting youth audiences who constitute a central part of the multiplex market. He saw *Trainspotting*'s soundtrack as crucial to this wider appeal (see Style: Music). His role as producer included supervising the complex process of securing the rights to all the music in the film. At the same time, he wanted to produce a film which could be taken seriously as more than just a showcase for its soundtrack (see Critical Responses).

Although *Trainspotting* was funded by television, director Danny Boyle aspired to make a film people would definitely want to see in the cinema. For him, films commissioned by television are often constrained by a realist style. In his opinion, this style may suit television but it doesn't always seem big or exciting enough for a cinema screening (see Style: Cinematography). Boyle wanted to ensure *Trainspotting* would work on the big as well as small screen by, for example, incorporating sets which gave the film a larger than life quality (see Style: Production Design).

Polygram's marketing budget and the production team's involvement in publicising *Trainspotting* made prospective audiences aware that a distinctive film would be arriving soon in British cinemas. In mid-1995, representatives from multiplex chains such as UCI and Showcase, as well as the art house cinema, the Gate at Notting Hill, were invited to visit *Trainspotting*'s set and view work in progress. Journalists writing for film and youth style magazines such as *Empire* and *ID* were also invited to visit the set. The aim was to build anticipation for the film's February 1996 release and ensure wide coverage by making cinema exhibitors and film reviewers feel involved in the project (see Critical Responses).

marketing

Polygram used much of *Trainspotting*'s marketing budget to commission high profile trailers and posters. These advertising campaigns gathered pace as the release date approached. *Trainspotting*'s posters were produced in several different versions. The basic design featured black and white images of Renton, Begbie, Diane, Sick Boy and Spud against white backgrounds. Numbers #1 to #5 plus their names were superimposed in orange over each character. Diane's presence indicated *Trainspotting* would feature an attractive woman and was not a film exclusively about men (see Cultural Contexts: New Lads).

An orange strip with the title *Trainspotting* in white lettering inside it appeared along the side or bottom of the posters. Text on the posters was kept to a minimum. Some versions of the poster featured individual characters and some featured all five pasted next to each other. Elements of this design and particularly the image of Ewan McGregor as Renton were used in the packaging of *Trainspotting*'s two soundtrack CDs, the cover of the reprint of Irvine Welsh's novel, the cover of the screenplay and the packaging of the video and DVD release versions of the film.

The basic poster design was memorable and intriguing because of its apparent simplicity. It did not reveal much about the film. Instead, its indirectness evoked a range of connotations for viewers, encouraging them to develop their own desire to see the film, rather than being explicitly told what it would be like. Black and white images are rarely used in contemporary film posters since they might imply the film itself is in black and white. Stylo Rouge, the design company responsible for creating *Trainspotting*'s poster, felt this was a risk worth taking because it emphasised the film's uniqueness. White backgrounds are usually associated with comedies because the colour implies light subject matter. In *Trainspotting*'s case, this connotation could offset reservations potential audiences might have about the possible grimness of a film dealing with heroin users.

Trainspotting's poster suggested a character-led film (see Narrative & Form: Character) and the design echoed advertising for *Reservoir Dogs* (Quentin Tarantino, 1992). The *Reservoir Dogs'* characters were introduced by a name superimposed over their image and blood red lettering was used. In *Trainspotting*'s poster, the characters' confidently humorous and aggressive facial expressions similarly established them as possessing attitude and style (see Genre). Their stares and gestures towards the poster's viewer indicated a dynamic, 'in your face' quality.

Representing the characters separately or pasted next to each other implied that while the film is concerned with a group of characters, it will also deal with divisions between them. None of the characters are involved in a narrative action or associated with a prop, such as a kiss for a romance or a gun for an action film. This avoided tying *Trainspotting* to one particular genre (see Genre). The poster does not locate the characters in any specific place (see Cultural Contexts: Representing Scotland). Despite their dynamic poses the characters are nowhere, frozen in time doing nothing in particular (see Narrative & Form: Chronology and Space).

Karen Lury, in her essay 'Here and Then: Space, Place and Nostalgia in British Youth Cinema of the 1990s', argues that, beyond these connotations, the key point about the *Trainspotting* phenomenon was that it became a successful brand which parodied the whole idea of branding. From the 1980s onwards, branded clothing, footwear and other consumer items have played an increasingly important role within Britain, especially British youth culture. During this period, consumers' critical awareness of branding's power as a marketing tool designed to maximise profits has also increased.

Hollywood films, most famously the *Star Wars* series, can establish profitable brand identities which help sell a whole range of products. A central aspect of the *Trainspotting* phenomenon was that it sold posters,

the characters as commodities

the film itself, two CD soundtracks, videos, DVDs, copies of the film script, the reprinted source novel and other associated merchandise. Yet it also questioned, in certain respects, the capitalist consumer culture which helped make it such a success (see Narrative & Form: Opening/Close and Industrial).

The *Trainspotting* phenomenon pushed to an extreme and pastiched the notion of branding while simultaneously branding everything associated with the film as distinctive, new and appealing. As Lury points out, the poster's numbering of characters emphasised their role as commodities. Audiences could 'collect' them by buying into the *Trainspotting* phenomenon. The *Trainspotting* title strip along the side or bottom of the posters not only advertised the film but also, by resembling the spine of the newly reprinted *Trainspotting* book and the edge of the soundtrack CDs, directed consumers towards associated products. The basic white design of the posters echoed the own-brand packaging used by some British supermarkets. The orange numbering and lettering was similar to that used in pharmaceutical packaging.

The way the *Trainspotting* phenomenon pastiched branding while simultaneously establishing itself as a brand is exemplified by the trailer which began to appear in cinemas in the run up to the film's release date. The main trailer featured Renton's opening 'Choose Life' monologue with the swearing bleeped out. It positioned the film as controversial yet humorous. It was also an advert for a film which, through its opening and closing 'Choose Life' monologues, raises questions about – but cannot see a way out of – the capitalist consumer culture advertising, branding and marketing are part of (see Narrative & Form: Opening/Close).

ideology: post-thatcherism

The Conservative Party governed Britain from 1979 until 1997. Margaret Thatcher was prime minister from 1979 to 1990. Her government broke with the more moderate consensus politics which preceding British

a radical right-wing agenda

governments had adhered to. 'Thatcherism' involved a radical new right-wing political agenda. Some of Thatcherism's ideological commitments and policies included:

■ A conviction that market forces rather than government regulation should drive the economy because this would eventually generate more prosperity for everyone. Private enterprise and competitive individualism were promoted as values which enriched society as a whole

■ An emphasis on British workers becoming more flexible to suit the needs of a changing economy driven by market forces. This led, for example in the miners' strike of 1984–5, to major conflicts with sectors of the workforce in industries deemed to be uneconomic. It also led to an abandonment of the commitment, maintained by previous British governments, to achieving full employment

■ A redefinition of the British public as consumers who should be free to make their own choices about how to spend their money. Measures such as the reduction of income tax were justified in these terms

■ A belief that people should take individual responsibility for the care of themselves and their families rather than relying upon state support. Government spending in areas such as social services, health care, education and housing was reduced. People were encouraged to provide for themselves in these areas through private health care and insurance policies, pension schemes, etc

A significant number of 1980s' British films were, broadly speaking, anti-Thatcherite. Many leading British film makers, such as Stephen Frears, Derek Jarman and Ken Loach, held left-wing, radical or liberal views formed in the very different political and cultural climate of the 1960s. During the 1980s, Thatcherism's precepts were not universally accepted. There was considerable resistance to them from certain sectors of British society. Thatcherism was not particularly popular with Britain's film makers, artists and intellectuals because its emphasis upon market forces and private enterprise extended into their areas of work. Government policy during the Thatcher era regarded artistic and cultural activities, including cinema, primarily as commercial concerns. Support structures and state subsidies for film production which had previously existed were removed or reduced.

Many 1980s' British films can be identified as anti-Thatcherite. In *Letter to Brezhnev* (Chris Bernard, 1985) a woman from Liverpool follows her Russian lover to the Soviet Union to escape from drabness, unemployment and poverty in Britain. *Sammy and Rosie Get Laid* (Stephen Frears, 1987) represents 1980s' London as an urban battleground, devastated by Conservative neglect, heavy-handed policing and the greed of property developers. It also explores how new social connections between diverse groups within the city might lead to alternatives to Thatcherism.

The Last of England (Derek Jarman, 1987) is bleaker than *Sammy and Rosie Get Laid*. It represents a disintegrating society and a widening gulf between rich and poor. *High Hopes* (Mike Leigh, 1988) contrasts competitive individualism and self-centred consumerism with socialist values of concern for and responsibility towards other people. *Riff-Raff* (Ken Loach, 1991) critiques the Thatcherite emphasis upon a flexible workforce. It is set on a building site where workers are endangered by inadequate safety precautions and fired for daring to confront their bosses.

Thatcher was replaced as prime minister by John Major in 1990, but by then Thatcherism was firmly entrenched within British culture. By the mid-1990s, much of the previous decade's resistance to Thatcherism had dissipated. To a certain extent the new Labour government elected in 1997 sought to emphasise a break with the past. It promised to reverse some consequences of Thatcherism, for example the decline of the National Health Service. The new Labour government's 're-branding' project, designed to challenge negative or backward-looking images of Britain, also implied that a new era in British history had arrived. At the same time, this re-branding project repackaged rather than rejected many elements of Thatcherism. These include its emphasis upon a flexible workforce and its celebration of 'enterprise culture' (see Background: Reading *Trainspotting*).

In *Trainspotting*, Renton's voice-over states, shortly after arriving in London, that there is no such thing as society and even if there were, he would have nothing to do with it. This is one of the few specific historical references in the narrative. Renton alludes to one of the most infamous statements Thatcher made during her period in office: 'There is no such thing as society. There are only individual men and women, and there are families.' *Trainspotting* contains exterior shots devoid of passers-by. These represent a world in which there is literally 'no such thing as society' (see Style: Cinematography). Renton's job as an estate agent in London involves selling people private space for themselves and their families. In the 1980s, this began to be perceived as a quintessentially Thatcherite occupation.

Trainspotting differs from *Sammy and Rosie Get Laid* in so far as Renton does not forge any new social connections in London. Instead, Renton betrays former friends in an enterprising act of competitive individualism. *Riff-Raff*'s narrative ends with the defiant, perhaps futile gesture of the builders burning down the site they have just converted from a hospital into luxury flats. *Trainspotting* opens with a gesture of defiance but this is inverted by the end of the narrative (see Narrative & Form: Opening/Close). None of *Trainspotting*'s characters even dream of escaping to somewhere better, as in *Letter to Brezhnev* (see Narrative & Form: Space). Unlike the 1980s' films discussed above, *Trainspotting* does not explore social, economic or political history, and there is no intimation of a future which might be different (see Background: Reading *Trainspotting*). It implies, like it or not, things are how they are and will remain that way.

Karen Lury (2000) argues that *Trainspotting*'s characters are poachers rather than rebels. Rebels challenge the status quo, often with a view to changing it. Poachers survive by adapting to the circumstances they operate within. They mark out their own paths within an environment they do not control and do not aspire to change.

Narrative events tend to happen to characters in *Trainspotting* rather than characters causing them to happen (see Narrative & Form: Character: Episodic Narration). For example, Spud is forced to attend a job interview. As a poacher his aim is to obtain what he wants from the situation by ensuring he fails the interview yet stays on the dole. Spud has no interest in challenging or changing the social order which puts him in this position. He just wants to extract what he can from it.

cultural contexts

the way the world inevitably works

Renton is not concerned with the rights or wrongs of becoming an estate agent in an overpriced London housing market. He simply enjoys the fact that he is flexible enough to adapt to this new role. *Trainspotting*, produced in the mid-1990s, differs from 1980s' anti-Thatcherite films. It can be categorised as a post-Thatcherite film. *Trainspotting* is post-Thatcherite in the sense that it does not necessarily endorse Thatcherite values but does not reject them either. It takes them for granted as the way the world inevitably works.

At the end of *Trainspotting*, Renton seems to accommodate himself to a conventional lifestyle and mainstream forms of consumerism. The ending can be seen as implying cynicism on Renton's part and as raising questions about the viability of the consumerist values he now apparently endorses (see Narrative & Form: Opening/Close). Like the film's marketing, the embrace of consumerism at the end of *Trainspotting* is therefore double-edged (see Marketing). Thatcherism vigorously promoted consumerism as something which would improve the quality of people's lives and give them more freedom. Aspects of the *Trainspotting* phenomenon hint at the possibility that this might be a rather shallow assumption. However, nowhere within the *Trainspotting* phenomenon is anything more profound on offer.

cultural contexts

NEW LADS

A new model of masculinity emerged in 1990s' British culture. Television series such as *Men Behaving Badly* (1990–1998) and glossy men's lifestyle magazines such as *loaded* (launched in 1994), *GQ* (1989), *FHM* (1994) and *Maxim* (1995) popularised the idea of the 'new lad'. Male style is crucial to these magazines. Much of their advertising is for branded clothing and male beauty products. Photographs of glamorous semi-naked women feature prominently on their covers and inside. Articles discuss male style, grooming, attitude and a cluster of stereotypically male interests such as football, sex, pub and club culture, violence and cars.

The new lad is a post-feminist model of masculinity. It emerged partly in

cultural contexts

sex, football and drugs

response to feminist criticisms, in the decades preceding the 1990s, of male identities defined in terms of stereotypical masculine pursuits and attitudes. New laddism implicitly acknowledges the existence of these feminist criticisms. It rejects them by implying that the new lad is essentially what men are, and that they cannot or will not change. In addition, it deflects criticism by apparently not taking itself too seriously. New lad attitudes are often characterised by irony and cynical humour, summed up in the front cover line describing *loaded* as a magazine 'for men who should know better'.

Claire Monk (2000) suggests *Trainspotting* owed some of its success to new lad appeal. The film deftly links together several new lad preoccupations. The **cut**, in the opening sequence, between Renton falling backwards after being hit on the head by a football and falling backwards from a hit of heroin links two new lad pleasures: football and drugs (see Style: Editing). Similarly, sex and football are linked throughout the narrative. Early in the narrative, Renton steals a home video of Tommy and Lizzy having sex and replaces it with a '100 great goals' tape. The two activities are made to seem synonymous and Renton later compares scoring with Diane to scoring a goal.

The consequences of Renton's theft of the video tape are played out in a sequence which **crosscuts** between couples having sex in three different locations: Diane and Renton; Lizzy and Tommy and Gail and Spud. Tommy and Lizzy play what they expect to be their home video. The video footage of a great goal being scored, with a commentary by Archie MacPherson laden with double entendres, is crosscut with shots of Renton and Diane climaxing (see Narrative & Form: Narration: Unrestricted Narration and Style: Editing). Renton identifies the goal Tommy and Lizzy have just screened, showing Archie Gemmill scoring against Holland in 1978.

With its male-centred narrative, humour, representations of violence, emphasis on style and linking together of sex, football and drugs, *Trainspotting* was well reviewed by new lad publications. The consensus was, as *GQ*'s review declared, that 'director Danny Boyle needs no tips on style'. In addition to supportive reviews like this, certain aspects of

60 TRAINSPOTTING **Y**

cultural contexts

a straightforward piece of new laddism

the marketing of the *Trainspotting* phenomenon reinforced its new lad appeal. The packaging of the first *Trainspotting* soundtrack CD quotes Renton's post-coital celebration of Archie Gemmill's goal. Although Diane's pose in the film poster is just as confident as the male characters', she is leaning forward to reveal her cleavage (see Marketing). The promise this implies is delivered when she appears naked in the film (see Style: Fashion).

Many aspects of the *Trainspotting* phenomenon encouraged its reception as a straightforward piece of new laddism, but there are other elements within it which point in different directions. Although they are not central to the narrative, the young women who appear in the film such as Lizzy, Gail and particularly Diane are confident and assertive. In the crosscut sex and football sequence, it is they who initiate each of the sexual encounters. Renton, like Diane, is completely naked in this sequence. Yet although both actors' bodies are on show, Kelly Macdonald's is more clearly marked through **point-of-view shots** as something to be looked at (see Background: Key Players' Biographies).

New laddism was very much in the ascendant during the 1990s, but other models of masculinity also circulated and became more visible within British culture during this period. Different types of gay and bisexual male identities and relationships were represented in British films as diverse as *Young Soul Rebels* (Isaac Julien, 1991), *Four Weddings and a Funeral* and *Love is the Devil* (John Maybury, 1998).

The Crying Game's (Neil Jordan, 1992) narrative begins with a caring relationship between an IRA gunman and a British soldier. It traces the developing relationship between the gunman and the soldier's transsexual girlfriend. *Trainspotting*, for all its new laddism, also incorporates an understated, caring male friendship, between Renton and Spud, and features a moment of sexual identity confusion. These elements in *Trainspotting* are nowhere near as central or as prominent as in *The Crying Game*, but are nevertheless there.

Renton and Begbie go to a London club. Renton's voice-over muses about dancers of indeterminate sexuality, saying that even men and women are becoming the same, a fact he is happy about.

representations of masculinity

This view differs from new laddism's fixed ideas of what real men are like. Begbie goes outside with a woman. To his horror, he discovers she is a transsexual. Renton's voice-over says there should be no problem with this, unless you're Begbie. Begbie agonises about his encounter in Renton's flat. Renton smirks and says Begbie could have enjoyed it. Begbie pins Renton to the wall and threatens to cut him up if he ever mentions it again.

This is the first time Begbie's violence is directed towards any of the other major male characters within *Trainspotting*'s narrative. After this, his behaviour becomes less humorous and more frightening. Begbie's threat marks another stage in Renton's reevaluation of his friendships within the all-male group he has previously been associated with (see Narrative & Form: Character: The Boundary Situation). Another link between Renton and Spud is that they both suffer physically from being around Begbie. Spud's hand is inadvertently slashed by Begbie's knife towards the end of the narrative when he tries to restrain him from knifing someone in a pub. Renton leaving a share of the drug deal money for Spud is a final expression of friendship over his betrayal of the other characters (see Narrative & Form: Character: Parallelism).

Trainspotting incorporates many new lad elements but also develops some more nuanced representations of masculinity. Renton is the character the spectator is closely linked to for most of the film (see Narrative & Form: Narration: Restricted Narration). During the London club sequence, his voice-over explores definitions of masculinity which begin to move beyond the constraints of new laddism. His comments open up a critical distance from the purely destructive masculinity Begbie embodies. What would have made *Trainspotting*'s representations of masculinity more adventurous would be if Renton's actions in the narrative had matched his voice-over comments; if he, rather than Begbie, had stepped outside the club with a transsexual.

DRUG DEBATES

Trainspotting, a film representing some of the pleasures of heroin use, inevitably courted controversy. It was not the first controversial film

cultural contexts

funded by Channel 4, a television channel created to provide space for non-mainstream perspectives (see Industrial). *My Beautiful Launderette* (Stephen Frears, 1985) surprised some commentators with its representation of a kiss between a white and Asian man. *Hidden Agenda* (Ken Loach, 1990) attracted harsh criticism from Conservative MPs for representing the conflict in Northern Ireland from a radical socialist perspective.

One cultural context relevant to *Trainspotting* was a shift in attitudes towards illegal drug use within British culture during the late 1980s and 1990s. This was related to the widespread popularity of ecstasy as a recreational drug. Rather than blanket condemnation of all illegal drug use, the need for rational debate on this issue began to be acknowledged. This was particularly the case with ecstasy and cannabis. This shift in attitudes developed to a point where, in October 2000, seven Conservative shadow cabinet ministers publicly admitted to having smoked cannabis at some point in the past.

The *Trainspotting* phenomenon made a provocative contribution to this cultural shift. It generated debate through its representation of the pleasures of heroin use. Renton's opening voice-over acknowledges debate and different views by stating that he knows about the bad side, but also enjoys it too.

Dialogue spoken by characters in the opening sequence articulates different points of view within this debate. Allison says heroin is better than sex. Tommy's comment is that it is a poison and a waste of life. Begbie sups a pint and smokes a cigarette while saying he'd never use illegal drugs. Renton's voice-over points out that his mother, prescribed Valium by her doctor, is in her own way also a drug addict. What is not included within *Trainspotting*'s range of debate is the economic and social contexts different types of legal and illegal drug use takes place within (see Background: Reading *Trainspotting* and Ideology: Post-Thatcherism).

Trainspotting's focus on heroin, a hard drug acknowledged to be much more dangerous than ecstasy or cannabis, concentrated on one of the most controversial areas of 1990s' drug debates. The production team conducted research into heroin culture. They protected themselves from

heroin culture

potential accusations of exploiting the issue by actively involving the Calton Athletic Centre in Glasgow. This centre for recovering addicts helped the team with their research and in return was given a small profit-share in the film. The BBFC (British Board of Film Classification) gave *Trainspotting* an 18 certificate but did not recommend any cuts in the cinema release version. The film was released only a few months after the much publicised case of Leah Betts' death after taking ecstasy at her eighteenth birthday party. This intensified critical debate about *Trainspotting*'s representations of drug use.

Film reviewers across the spectrum of British newspapers and magazines adopted different stances on *Trainspotting*'s representations of drug use. One criticism was that the film's dynamism and its makers' aspiration to engage a wide audience trivialised the seriousness of heroin use (see Production History). Tom Shone, writing in the *Sunday Times* (1996), was not impressed by *Trainspotting*'s 'street poetry' or its 'finger-snapping' editing. For him, its 'indiscriminate regard for the Spunky Spirit of Renegade Youth' made it a virtual advert for heroin, 'the film about drugs that likes to say "YES!"'.

Some reviewers writing for conservative tabloid newspapers were concerned about the impact *Trainspotting* would have on its audiences. Edward Verity, writing in the *Daily Mail* (1996), suggested that Renton's survival and apparent good health at the end of the film would send out the wrong moral message to *Trainspotting*'s youth audiences. Reservations were expressed in some specialist film magazines as well. *Premiere*'s Ryan Gilbey (1996) felt that *Trainspotting*'s comedy and dynamic pace prevented its representations of the negative consequences of drug taking in the latter part of the narrative from acquiring any real weight. For him, these aspects of the film outweighed the change of tone in the latter part of the narrative (see Narrative & Form: Little Hits Of Sensation and Character: The Boundary Situation).

Other film reviewers emphasised *Trainspotting*'s more sombre representations of heroin use. In the broadsheet *The Observer* (1996), Philip French argued that *Trainspotting* could not be accused of glamorising heroin when some of its negative consequences, such as Tommy's death and Renton's overdose, were so graphically represented. *Empire*'s Neil Jeffries (1996) emphasised the narrative's 'stunning turnaround', its change in tone after baby Dawn dies (see Narrative & Form: Character: The Boundary Situation). For him, only one conclusion could be drawn from this aspect of *Trainspotting*'s narrative structure: '... it all goes pear-shaped, naturally, and no one is surprised, because by now the message is sinking in: heroin is for losers.'

What Jeffries did concede was that *Trainspotting* could be differently received in different contexts. His comments about the effect of the 'stunning turnaround' were made in a review of the video release of the film. He suggested that watching *Trainspotting* at home tended to produce a different response from watching it in a cinema where collective enjoyment of the film's comic moments might predominate over serious reflection upon the negative consequences of heroin use. *Trainspotting*'s representations of heroin use are open to a range of different interpretations and responses. These will vary depending on who is watching the film and the different contexts in which it is screened (see Audience).

Reviewers who argued that *Trainspotting* was either moral or immoral, responsible or irresponsible in its representations of heroin use tend to focus selectively on certain aspects of its narrative structure and style while ignoring others. The range of film reviewers' responses to *Trainspotting* confirms Susan Corrigan's observation in the youth magazine *ID* (1996) that the film carried no consistent 'moral message about the lives of its characters or the drugs they use.' *Trainspotting*'s moral inconsistency is compatible with the broader context of drug debates in 1990s' British culture. To condemn illegal drug use outright, to represent it only as a social problem and users simply as victims would have been seen, particularly by many youth audiences, as out of step with the times (see Audience).

As Neil Jeffries pointed out, it is not just films themselves but also the contexts surrounding them which need to be taken into account when analysing their representations of particular issues. Marketing constructed an immediate context which underplayed *Trainspotting*'s representations of the negative consequences of heroin use and foregrounded its humour and style instead. In the film, the opportunistic, adaptable, stylish Renton survives addiction right in the middle of an epidemic. Ewan McGregor's image as Renton was central to *Trainspotting*'s marketing. The honest, innocent, emotionally vulnerable Tommy is the one major character who dies in the film. His image was conspicuously absent from *Trainspotting*'s poster campaign (see Marketing).

REPRESENTING SCOTLAND

Trainspotting's success raises questions about national and cultural identity. In cultural terms, *Trainspotting*'s credentials as a Scottish film seem clear. It was adapted from a book by a Scottish writer, shot in Scotland, produced and written by Scots and featured Scottish actors. However, in economic terms, it can be defined as a British film. Its production funding came directly from Channel 4, a London-based rather than specifically Scottish source (see Industrial).

Trainspotting's production and distribution is best understood within the larger context of British cinema. It is similar in this respect to *Four Weddings and a Funeral*, set mainly in England, and *The Crying Game*, which begins in Northern Ireland. *Trainspotting* must also be understood in relation to a wider transnational context. One of the production team's aims was to construct a film which would appeal, particularly to youth audiences, throughout and beyond Britain (see Production History).

Certain stereotypical **representations** of Scotland have tended to find favour with cinema audiences outside Scotland. 'Tartanry' has proved very popular, a term derived from the tartan plaid designs supposedly worn by traditional Scots to denote the clan they belong to. Tartanry involves a romantic representation of Scotland. It focuses on the past, on imagined, colourful Scottish traditions and legendary, tragic battles in which proud Scots are defeated after struggling valiantly against the English. Films of this type usually display awesome Scottish landscapes as a point of appeal for their audiences. Their heroes are rugged, charismatic men, their heroines alluring, independent women. Two 1990s' examples are *Rob Roy* (Michael Caton-Jones, 1995) and *Braveheart* (Mel Gibson, 1996).

cultural contexts

An alternative, even opposing type of representation is 'Clydesideism'. The term refers to an area of Glasgow with a tough reputation. Clydesideism focuses on violent hard men within more contemporary Scottish urban environments. Alcohol, football and industrial labour – or the lack of it – are key elements here. Films incorporating aspects of Clydesideism include *The Big Man* (David Leland, 1990) and *The Near Room* (David Hayman, 1995).

Trainspotting assumes its audiences are likely to have some familiarity with Tartanry and Clydesideism. It draws upon this familiarity to distance itself from these ways of representing Scotland. Tartanry is savagely attacked when Tommy unwisely drags Renton, Sick Boy and Spud to go for a walk in the 'great outdoors'. This moment is memorable because it is the only one where the narrative action moves away from interiors to a rural exterior. The scenery is typical of Tartanry's emphasis upon romantic Scottish landscapes. In an **extreme long shot**, with impressive greenery and hills behind him, Tommy innocently explains how these surroundings make him proud to be Scottish. Renton's angry retort is delivered mainly in **close-up**, when he says that fresh air doesn't make up for the fact that, for him, the Scottish are the lowest of the low, colonised by the 'effete' English.

As far as Renton is concerned, romantic nonsense about the 'great outdoors' is a form of consolation for Scotland's subordination to England. He savagely attacks Tommy's naïve endorsement of Tartanry. At one point during Renton's diatribe, there is a cut back to Tommy in extreme long shot then back to Renton in close-up. The dramatic change of shot size underlines their sharp difference of opinion.

The representation of Scotland in *Trainspotting* could be seen as closer to Clydesideism. Scottish football culture is referred to, albeit briefly, at several points in the narrative (see Cultural Contexts: New Lads). Some of the film's interiors are pubs where violence occurs. Yet *Trainspotting* complicates this representation in several ways. Clydesideism is primarily associated with Glasgow. Edinburgh, with its historic castle and magnificent views, is commonly associated with Tartanry. The Scottish sections of *Trainspotting*'s narrative, set in Edinburgh, challenge this

cultural contexts

convention.

This challenge to conventions becomes painfully acute for an unwitting middle-aged American tourist who gets mugged by Begbie and the others. He enters a pub they are drinking in on the first day of the Edinburgh festival. Expecting Tartanry, he encounters something closer to Clydesideism. At the same time, *Trainspotting* subtly distances itself from straightforward Clydesideism. Begbie, the stereotypically violent hard man, is marked by the clothes he wears as less stylish and less representative of youth culture than the other characters (see Style: Fashion). Later in the narrative, Renton's voice-over suggests his attitudes are outdated (see Cultural Contexts: New Lads).

International audiences can connect with *Trainspotting* through the way it plays with the conventions of Tartanry and Clydesideism. It acknowledges these expectations but does something different with them. This tactic combines with elements which deliberately work against making *Trainspotting* seem too Scottish, too nationally or culturally specific and therefore of limited interest to outsiders. Stylisation opens the film up to international audiences. Many of *Trainspotting*'s interiors could be located anywhere. Fashion, production design and cinematography construct a stylised world rather than a specific social environment (see Style: Fashion, Production Design and Cinematography). The soundtrack's mixture of American and British music orientates the film towards international audiences (see Style: Music).

Colin McArthur, in his essay 'The Cultural Necessity of a Poor Celtic Cinema', develops a polemical argument about Scottish film production. He insists there should be more film making in Scotland geared primarily towards Scottish audiences. To be economically viable, budgets for this type of production must be kept extremely low; no more than £300,000 at mid-1990s prices, far less than the £1.7 million allocated to *Trainspotting*. Otherwise, even low-budget feature films such as *Trainspotting* are likely to steer away from engaging with the specificities and complexities of Scottish culture. This is because, within the context of 1990s' British film production, even low-budget film making will be geared towards wider, non-Scottish audiences (see Industrial). These audiences' understanding of

an artificial version of Scottish culture

or interest in Scottish culture is likely to be minimal, or limited to stereotypical representations such as Tartanry and Clydesideism.

Trainspotting excises the more local aspects of its source novel for the sake of wider accessibility (see Background: Key Players' Biographies: Screenwriter's Adaptation). For a critic such as McArthur, this would be counted as a loss. However, there is one area of complexity, discussed by Murray Smith in his essay 'Transnational Trainspotting', which both insiders and outsiders can relate to. This is the interaction between local and global elements within *Trainspotting*'s representation of contemporary Scottish urban youth culture. These are fused to the point where it is sometimes impossible to disentangle them. For example, the characters know and care much more about American musicians Iggy Pop and Lou Reed than they do about the Scottish countryside (see Style: Music). These and other American influences form a central part of the characters' experience of contemporary Scottish culture.

Spud complains it is not natural when Tommy suggests he, Renton and Sick Boy embrace Tartanry by going for a walk in the countryside. Tartanry is denounced as an artificial version of Scottish culture. What comes 'naturally' to *Trainspotting*'s characters is an acceptance of their culture and their experiences as simultaneously local and global. The best example of this is Sick Boy's obsessive references to Sean Connery. Connery is a local cultural hero who is also globally recognisable. He is an Edinburgh boy made good as well as a major Hollywood star. He is both an international icon and a tax exile who supports Scottish nationalism. His star image reaches out to wider audiences but carries particular meanings for Scots. Non-Scottish audiences can relate to Sick Boy's obsession even if they are not fully aware of Sean Connery's significance within contemporary Scottish culture.

genre

Genre has been analysed in a number of ways within film and media studies. In traditional approaches to genre study, individual films would often be evaluated in terms of how well they lived up to or deviated from classic examples of their genre. Alternatively, what was unique and specific to a particular genre film would be overlooked and only those elements it shared with other films within its genre would be studied. One problem with these approaches is that they cannot do justice to the complexities of genre history, especially when dealing with films such as *Trainspotting* which do not fit neatly into any one genre.

More recent critical approaches to genre pay close attention to how genres change and develop over time. Recent approaches to genre study are also interested in analysing how marketing, film reviewers, commentators and audiences have answered the question: 'What type of film is this?' Sarah Street (2000) points out that three loosely defined genres were cited as relevant to *Trainspotting*. These were the drug film, 'Swinging London' films and American independent and cult films.

TRAINSPOTTING AND DRUG FILMS

References were made, in media coverage of the *Trainspotting* phenomenon, to previous drug films. *Christiane F.* (Uli Edel, 1981), a film about a young German girl addicted to heroin, was often mentioned as a point of comparison. Although *Christiane F.* does attempt to explore its protagonist Christiane's subjectivity, for example when she listens to David Bowie's music, it represents heroin addicts primarily as victims. Christiane suffers and her life descends into degradation, but she finally manages to come off heroin. Reviewers tended to note these differences between *Christiane F.* and *Trainspotting*.

Drugstore Cowboy (Gus Van Sant, 1989) was sometimes mentioned as being closer in narrative structure and style to *Trainspotting*. *Drugstore Cowboy* represents the pleasures of drug taking through short sequences where floating objects or specks of light are superimposed upon close-ups of protagonist Bob's face and shots of clouds. Bob's voice-over opens and closes the film. Another similarity to *Trainspotting* is that one character of a group of friends dies halfway through the narrative as a result of her drug taking. Despite these similarities, *Drugstore Cowboy* is more melancholy and less humorous than *Trainspotting*. The narrative begins and ends with Bob lying in an ambulance after having been shot by an acquaintance.

Trainspotting production team members, when interviewed, emphasised that their film was not only about drugs and should not be understood solely in relation to previous drug films. In this respect, their comments paralleled the film's marketing, which also underplayed this element (see Marketing and Cultural Contexts: Drug Debates). Efforts were made to relate *Trainspotting* to more light-hearted and pleasurable genres and to films which had status and credibility with contemporary youth audiences. One light-hearted group of British films that *Trainspotting* was linked to was the Swinging London cycle of the 1960s.

SWINGING LONDON CYCLE

Films considered part of the Swinging London cycle include *A Hard Day's Night* (Richard Lester, 1963), *The Knack* (Richard Lester, 1965) and *Alfie* (Lewis Gilbert, 1966). Set in London, they focus on the fun, freedom and excitement of 1960s' youth. They incorporate comic elements and place a lot of emphasis upon style. When *The Knack* was first released, its production design, cinematography and editing were seen as new and different from previous British realist films. *Trainspotting* similarly breaks with stylistic realism (see Style: Production Design and Cinematography). *Alfie* established its star, Michael Caine, as a style icon. *Trainspotting* did the same for Ewan McGregor (see Background: Key Players' Biographies). All of the Swinging London films, especially the first Beatles' film, *A Hard Day's Night*, included pop music on their soundtracks.

The Internet Movie Database listed 'trivia points' linking *Trainspotting* to *A Hard Day's Night*. Shots of Renton and Spud running towards the camera away from store detectives in *Trainspotting*'s opening sequence are reminiscent of *A Hard Day's Night*'s opening sequence. In this film, the Beatles run towards the camera away from adoring fans. *Alfie*, like *Trainspotting*, employs restricted narration and ends in a similar location with Alfie walking along the Embankment near a London bridge (see Narrative & Form: Narration: Restricted Narration and Style: Cinematography). In *Trainspotting*, Renton's transition to London is represented through a playful **montage sequence** including shots of Big Ben, Trafalgar Square, Carnaby Street and a red London bus. The production team designed this as an affectionate pastiche of similar sequences in several Swinging London films.

Emphasising the influence of Swinging London films helped position *Trainspotting* as a lively, energetic film which was as much about youth, fun and fashion as about drugs. Producer Andrew Macdonald made it clear the Swinging London cycle was the only British film tradition he wanted *Trainspotting* to be compared to when he told an interviewer: 'I think that was the last period when Britain actually made films about contemporary subjects that were exciting and impactful' (Macnab, *Sight and Sound*, February 1996).

AMERICAN INDEPENDENT AND CULT FILMS

Trainspotting was linked, both within the film itself and in commentary surrounding it, to the Swinging London cycle. At the same time connections to a wider range of predominantly American independent and cult films with a somewhat darker tone were also highlighted. At the Volcano club, the production design and a slow **tracking shot** towards Spud and Tommy mimics a similar moment in *A Clockwork Orange* (Stanley Kubrick, 1971). In *A Clockwork Orange*, the main characters speak their own invented language. When this film is alluded to in *Trainspotting*, subtitles translate Tommy's and Spud's conversation (see Narrative & Form: Narration: Voice-over).

Later in the Volcano club, Renton stands in front of a wall painting of Robert de Niro as Travis Bickle in *Taxi Driver* (Martin Scorsese, 1976). This reference wryly points up similarities and differences between Bickle's fixation with a very young woman and the sex-starved Renton who is about to encounter Diane. Renton's hallucinations when locked in his bedroom to come off heroin culminate with baby Dawn's head revolving before she falls towards him from the ceiling. This image derives from the cult film *The Exorcist* (William Friedkin, 1973), where the head of a child possessed by the devil revolves in a similar manner.

By the mid-1990s, *A Clockwork Orange*, *Taxi Driver* and *The Exorcist* had acquired a cult reputation as stylish, intense pieces of cinema which dealt with controversial and disturbing subject matter. *A Clockwork*

celebrating the pleasures of banned films

Orange and *Taxi Driver* are, like *Trainspotting*, examples of films which incorporate elements derived from art cinema (see Narrative & Form: Art Cinema Influences). *A Clockwork Orange* and *The Exorcist* were not legally available on video in Britain when *Trainspotting* was released. Association with them enhanced *Trainspotting*'s own reputation as a cult film. In addition to celebrating the pleasures of proscribed drugs, *Trainspotting* celebrates the pleasures of banned films.

Connections were also established between *Trainspotting* and more recent cult films. Director Danny Boyle often told journalists how impressed he had been with the possibilities opened up by the use of voice-over in *Goodfellas* (Martin Scorsese, 1990). He also praised Quentin Tarantino's films. *Trainspotting*'s use of popular music resembles the carefully organised soundtracks in films directed by Scorsese and Tarantino (see Style: Music).

Miramax, the company which distributed *Trainspotting* in America, had previously distributed the commercially successful *Pulp Fiction* (Quentin Tarantino, 1994) (see Industrial). Miramax's trailer for *Trainspotting* emphasised the drug deal towards the end of the narrative and the overall style of the film. Emphasising the drug deal as an objective for the characters within the narrative downplays the more unconventional aspects of *Trainspotting*'s narrative which mainstream audiences might be wary of (see Narrative & Form: Art Cinema Influences). Highlighting style and crime in *Trainspotting* also suggested the film would appeal to audiences who had enjoyed films directed by Tarantino.

Trainspotting deals with what could be seen as minority interest subject matter. Positioning it as a film drawing upon several genres particularly associated with youth audiences was crucial to broadening its appeal. *Trainspotting* was marked out as a new, less harrowing, less didactic type of drug film. References to Swinging London films linked *Trainspotting* to a type of British cinema perceived as fun and enjoyable, while references to popular contemporary independent and cult films helped establish *Trainspotting*'s appeal for fans of this type of cinema.

critical responses

Critical responses to *Trainspotting* were broadly favourable, for different reasons, in a diverse range of publications. Those finding fault with the film tended to concentrate on the issue of its representations of heroin use (see Cultural Contexts: Drug Debates). The extent and variety of the coverage *Trainspotting* received was partly a result of the high profile generated by the film's marketing (see Marketing). Press releases were issued and Andrew Macdonald, Danny Boyle, John Hodge and the actors made themselves available to talk to journalists both during production and as the film was being released. This ensured newspapers and specialist film and youth style magazines would be likely to give the *Trainspotting* phenomenon extensive coverage.

Reviewers in British youth style magazines generally appreciated what they perceived as the clued-up, unpatronising approach of *Trainspotting*'s production team. Reviewers in these magazines identified *Trainspotting* as the first 1990s' British film to connect with youth audiences through its style. *The Face*, *ID* and *Sky* devoted a lot of space to photographs of the actors and clothes worn in the film (see Style: Fashion). *The Face* (February 1996) quoted Jarvis Cocker, Pulp's lead singer, as saying: 'they've got [the soundtrack] right with *Trainspotting*' (see Style: Music). The film's stylistic departure from realism was also seen as important (see Style: Production Design and Cinematography). In *The Face* (February 1996), Irvine Welsh endorsed *Trainspotting*'s 'action and energy', qualities he felt British realist films lacked. In the same magazine, journalist Craig McLean praised *Trainspotting* for being 'as hip to style as it is to substance'.

Reviewers differed on exactly what they made of *Trainspotting*'s style. The main focus in *The Face*, *ID* and *Sky* was on *Trainspotting*'s sheer stylistic dynamism. Reviewers in more intellectual film magazines and broadsheet newspapers were keener to stress there was meaning behind the style. Philip Kemp in *Sight and Sound* (March 1996) argued *Trainspotting*'s style was appropriate to the 'hyped' characters and 'fractured' culture the film represents. The *Sunday Telegraph*'s film reviewer argued *Trainspotting*'s direction was 'rigorous, with not a skewed perspective ... out of place', and its stylistic invention 'gleeful, but always tailored to the material'. Emphasis was placed on the 'rigour' of the direction to reassure readers that *Trainspotting* was a serious film, with a reason for every aspect of the style, rather than a shallow exercise in style for its own sake.

audience

The fact that *Trainspotting* could be praised by reviewers in a variety of different publications was crucial to its crossover success (see Production History). As Xan Brooks (1998) puts it, *Trainspotting* 'defies easy classification'. This enabled reviewers to recommend the film to audiences with a range of different interests and expectations. *Trainspotting*'s style and narrative structure encompassed elements drawn from both music video and art cinema (see Narrative & Form: Little Hits Of Sensation and Art Cinema Influences).

A sophisticated, expensive marketing campaign and good reviews certainly helped bring *Trainspotting* to many people's attention, but its success and impact cannot be attributed to these factors alone (see Marketing). Other films have been vigorously marketed or well reviewed but have not generated the same level of audience response. Tangible evidence of this level of audience response can be found in various places. At one end of the spectrum are academics (see Bibliography) who consider the film important enough to analyse closely and write about at length. At the other end of the spectrum are the many fans who have set up *Trainspotting* websites. Although quite different to the academics, the work of this group also testifies to their close involvement with the film.

Academics might be more inclined to analyse the reasons for *Trainspotting*'s cultural significance, and fans more inclined to celebrate it, but the dividing line is not always clear. What is clear is that for 1990s' cinema goers, *Trainspotting* was a difficult film to be indifferent towards. The *Trainspotting* phenomenon excited, disturbed, provoked or intrigued various audiences. For many individuals, more than one of these responses might be felt simultaneously and might change over time.

Trainspotting became, as Xan Brooks puts it, a film 'synonymous with nineties British culture'. It translated certain aspects of wider drug debates into a cinematic format. It resonated with several other key issues within 1990s' British culture. These include the apparent permanence of Thatcherist values, the rise of new lad culture, changing representations of national identity, increasing commercialisation and the general pervasiveness of branding.

filmography

Trainspotting broke new ground, stylistically and culturally, within British cinema. Subsequent British films registered its influence and attempted to repeat its success. *Twin Town* (Kevin Allen, 1997), about underclass youth in Swansea, was produced by members of the *Trainspotting* team. *The Acid House* (Paul McGuigan, 1998) was another film based upon Irvine Welsh's fiction featuring *Trainspotting* actors Ewen Bremner and Kevin McKidd.

Polygram's marketing campaign for *Lock, Stock and Two Smoking Barrels* (Guy Ritchie, 1998) emphasised its new lad appeal. The poster carried a reviewer's recommendation comparing it to the 1960s' British film *The Italian Job* (Peter Collinson, 1969) as well as *Reservoir Dogs* (see Genre). *Human Traffic* (Justin Kerrigan, 1998) and *Saving Grace* (Nigel Cole, 2000) continued the project of translating aspects of wider drug debates into a cinematic format. These films represented characters enjoying ecstasy and cannabis respectively. *Human Traffic*'s energetic style was clearly indebted to *Trainspotting*, whose stylistic influence could even be detected in the costume dramas *Elizabeth* (Shekhar Kapur, 1998) and *Plunkett and Macleane* (Jake Scott, 1999), starring Robert Carlyle and Jonny Lee Miller.

Trainspotting also broke new ground industrially. Films such as *Trainspotting, Twin Town, Human Traffic, Lock, Stock and Two Smoking Barrels* and *Snatch* (Guy Ritchie, 2000) constitute a significant new trend within British cinema. They are low-budget films unapologetically aimed at multiplex youth audiences. This new orientation emerges from the industrial conditions prevailing within the British film industry in the latter part of the 1990s and into the new millennium (see Industrial).

filmography

Some commentators, such as Nick Roddick in his polemical article 'Show Me the Culture!', are concerned about the longer-term consequences of this situation. Roddick argues that the British film industry needs to be supported by a government policy which recognises that, although box office success is crucial to a healthy industry, all films cannot be evaluated by commercial criteria alone. Cultural criteria are also important. His concern is that an increasingly commercial emphasis provides fewer opportunities for the making of the aesthetically radical and politically oppositional, lower-budget British feature films that Channel 4 supported in the 1980s (see Industrial and Ideology: Post-Thatcherism).

Roddick's article is not a plea to turn the clock back. Things will never be quite the same again in British cinema after *Trainspotting*. Roddick's argument forms part of a larger debate about the industrial conditions which shaped *Trainspotting*. Even if *Trainspotting* is an outstandingly innovative film, these conditions might in the longer-term lead to a narrowing of British film culture. Roddick suggests that it might be necessary to try and steer the industry in a different direction in order to sustain a truly diverse film culture. This debate is the key one arising from a study of *Trainspotting*'s contexts, but it is also one which extends beyond the scope of this book. What is certain is that *Trainspotting* became British cinema's most historically important film of the 1990s.

bibliography

general film

Altman, Rick, *Film Genre*, BFI, 1999
Detailed exploration of the concept of film genre

Bordwell, David, *Narration in the Fiction Film*, Routledge, 1985
A detailed study of narrative theory and structures

– – –, Staiger, Janet & Thompson, Kristin, *The Classical Hollywood Cinema: Film Style & Mode of Production to 1960*, Routledge, 1985; pbk 1995
An authoritative study of cinema as institution, it covers film style and production

– – – & Thompson, Kristin, *Film Art*, McGraw-Hill, 4th edn, 1993
An introduction to film aesthetics for the non-specialist

Branson, Gill & Stafford, Roy, *The Media Student's Handbook*, Routledge, 2nd edn, 1999

Buckland, Warren, *Teach Yourself Film Studies*, Hodder & Stoughton, 1998
Very accessible, it gives an overview of key areas in film studies

Cook, Pam & Bernink, Mieke (eds), *The Cinema Book*, BFI, 2nd edn, 1999

Corrigan, Tim, *A Short Guide To Writing About Film*, HarperCollins, 1994
What it says: a practical guide for students

Dyer, Richard (with Paul McDonald), *Stars*, BFI, 2nd edn, 1998
A good introduction to the star system

Easthope, Antony, *Classical Film Theory*, Longman, 1993
A clear overview of writing about film theory

Hayward, Susan, *Key Concepts in Cinema Studies*, Routledge, 1996

Hill, John & Gibson, Pamela Church (eds), *The Oxford Guide to Film Studies*, Oxford University Press, 1998
Wide-ranging standard guide

Lapsley, Robert & Westlake, Michael, *Film Theory: An Introduction*, Manchester University Press, 1994

Maltby, Richard & Craven, Ian, *Hollywood Cinema*, Blackwell, 1995
A comprehensive work on the Hollywood industry and its products

Mulvey, Laura, 'Visual Pleasure and Narrative Cinema' (1974), in *Visual and Other Pleasures*, Indiana University Press, Bloomington, 1989
The classic analysis of 'the look' and 'the male gaze' in Hollywood cinema. Also available in numerous other edited collections

Nelmes, Jill (ed.), *Introduction to Film Studies*, Routledge, 2nd edn, 1999
Deals with several national cinemas and key concepts in film study

Nowell-Smith, Geoffrey (ed.), *The Oxford History of World Cinema*, Oxford University Press, 1996
Hugely detailed and wide-ranging with many features on 'stars'

TRAINSPOTTING **y**

Thomson, David, _A Biographical Dictionary of the Cinema_,
Secker & Warburg, 1975
   Unashamedly driven by personal taste, but often stimulating

Truffaut, François, _Hitchcock_,
Simon & Schuster, 1966,
rev. edn. Touchstone, 1985
   Landmark extended interview

Turner, Graeme, _Film as Social Practice_,
3rd edn, Routledge, 1999
   Chapter four, 'Film Narrative', discusses structuralist theories of narrative

Wollen, Peter, _Signs and Meaning in the Cinema_,
BFI 1997 (revised edn)
   An important study in semiology

Readers should also explore the many relevant websites and journals.

Film Education and _Sight and Sound_ are standard reading.

Valuable websites include:

The Internet Movie Database at www.uk.imdb.com

Screensite at www.tcf.ua.edu/screensite/contents.html

The Media and Communications Site at the University of Aberystwyth at www.aber.ac.uk/~dgc/welcome.html

There are obviously many other university and studio websites which are worth exploring in relation to film studies.

scottish & british cinema in the 1990s

Kennedy, Harlan, 'Kiltspotting: Highland Reels', in _Film Comment_ vol.32 no.4, July-August 1996
   An analysis of the style and themes of 1990s' Scottish films

McArthur, Colin, 'The Cultural Necessity of a Poor Celtic Cinema', in _Border Crossings: Film in Ireland, Britain and Europe_, John Hill, Martin McLoone and Paul Hainsworth (eds), BFI, 1994

A polemical argument about how Scottish cinema should be organised in order not to lose sight of specifically Scottish concerns

Roddick, Nick, 'Show Me the Culture!', in _Sight and Sound_ vol.8 no.12, December 1998
   A polemical argument about the state of the British film industry in the late 1990s and the type of film making this encourages

trainspotting

Lury, Karen, 'Here and Then: Space, Place and Nostalgia in British Youth Cinema of the 1990s', in *British Cinema of the 90s*, Robert Murphy (ed.), BFI, 2000
> Explores why *Trainspotting* was the most successful 1990s' British youth film

Monk, Claire, 'Men in the 90s', in *British Cinema of the 90s*, Robert Murphy (ed.), BFI, 2000
> Discusses *Trainspotting* in relation to new lad culture

Monk, Claire, 'Underbelly UK: the 1990s underclass film, masculinity and the ideologies of "new Britain"', in *British Cinema, Past and Present*, Justine Ashby and Andrew Higson (eds), Routledge, 2000
> Analyses *Trainspotting*'s ideological dimensions

Smith, Murray, 'Transnational Trainspotting', in *The Media in Britain*, Anna Reading and Jane Stokes (eds), Macmillan, 1999
> Analyses representations of national and transnational identity

Street, Sarah, '*Trainspotting*', in *European Cinema: An Introduction*, Jill Forbes and Sarah Street, Macmillan, 2000
> Discusses genre, marketing and reviews

trainspotting's production & marketing

Finney, Angus, *The State of European Cinema*, Cassell, 1996

Macnab, Geoffrey, 'Geoffrey Macnab Talks to the Team that Made *Trainspotting*', in *Sight and Sound* vol.6 no.2, February 1996

Thompson, Andrew O, 'Trains, Veins and Heroin Deals', in *American Cinematographer* vol.77 no.8, August 1996

Westbrook, Caroline, 'First Class Return', in *Empire*, March 1996

ewan mcgregor's star image

Brooks, Xan, *Choose Life: Ewan McGregor and the British Film Revival*, Chameleon Books, 1998

Street, Sarah, *British Cinema in Documents*, Routledge, 2000

reviews

source novel, screenplay, adaptation

Cardullo, Bert, 'Fiction into Film, or Bringing Welsh to a Boyle', in *Literature/Film Quarterly* vol.25 no.3, 1997

Hodge, John, *Trainspotting and Shallow Grave*, Faber, 1996

Welsh, Irvine, *Trainspotting*, Minerva, 1994 (first published 1993)

reviews cited in this note

Charity, Tom, 'The Other Side of the Tracks', in *Time Out*, 31 January-7 February 1996

Corrigan, Susan, 'Walking the Line', in *ID*, February 1996

French, Philip, '*Trainspotting* review', in *Observer Review*, 25 February 1996

Gilbey, Ryan, '*Trainspotting* review', in *Premiere*, March 1996

Jeffries, Neil, '*Trainspotting* video review', in *Empire*, September 1996

Kemp, Philip, '*Trainspotting* review', in *Sight and Sound*, vol.6 no.3, March 1996

McCabe, Doug, '*Trainspotting* review', in *GQ*, March 1996

McLean, Craig, 'Hey Hey! It's the Junkies', in *The Face*, February 1996

Rawsthorn, Alice, 'Polygram is marketing *Trainspotting* as the next cult hit with crossover appeal', in *Financial Times*, 27 January 1996

Self, Will, 'Carry on up the hypodermic', in *Observer Review*, 17 February 1996

Shone, Tom, 'Needle March', in *The Sunday Times Culture Supplement*, 25 February, 1996

'Trainspotting review', in *Sunday Telegraph*, 25 February 1996

Verity, Edward, '*Trainspotting* review', in *Daily Mail*, 9 February 1996

cinematic terms

camera height the camera can be positioned at different heights in relation to what is within the frame. For example, a camera could be positioned to film only the tops of characters' heads

close-up a shot framing someone's face, a gesture, or an object

cut an instantaneous transition between two shots

crosscut/crosscutting cutting back and forth between two or more different spaces

diegesis a film studies term for what exists within a film's narrative space (adjective: **diegetic**)

dissolve an editing device where the end of one shot is superimposed over the beginning of the next shot

ellipsis a narrative device which noticeably skips over a period of story time. A definite ellipsis occurs when the amount of story time eliminated can be more or less calculated; an indefinite one occurs when this is unclear

extreme close-up a shot magnifying a very small object, isolating a detail of an object, or isolating a part of someone's face such as the mouth, ears or eyes

extreme long shot a shot of a city or a landscape where human figures are barely distinguishable because of the size of what is included in the shot

eyeline match an aspect of continuity editing; helping the shots to make sense across cuts and joins by ensuring that eyes in one shot are looking in the correct direction to match logically with what they are supposed to be looking at

fade an editing device where a shot fades to black before the next shot begins, or a shot begins black and lightens to become perceptible

flashback a section of the narrative representing past events, usually linked to a particular character's recollection. The beginning and end of flashbacks have traditionally been indicated by the beginning or end of a voice-over, or optical effects such as a fade or a gradual dissolve

freeze frame an editing device where the moving image is frozen for a period of time

graphic match a link between successive shots based upon similar shapes, colours, types of lighting or movement in each shot

high angle shot a shot from a position looking down at what is within the frame

impossible camera position a shot from a position where no character or human observer could be located

interior monologue a term used in literary criticism. A technique used in novels which relates thoughts passing through a character's mind

jump cut if similar shots of the same subject are cut together, they can cause a jump on screen. Classical editing tends to follow the '30° rule'. This dictates that the camera angles of successive shots of the same subject should differ by at least 30°. If this rule is broken, a jump cut can occur because of the similarity between the shots

cinematic terms

long shot a shot where a person's entire body can be seen and where the background dominates

low angle shot a shot from a position looking up at what is within the frame

masked shot a shot where part of the frame is blocked out

match on action an action begun in one shot is matched in the next shot in order to reinforce the spectator's impression of coherent space and continuous time

medium close-up a shot framing the human body from the chest up

medium shot a shot framing the human body from the waist up

mise-en-scène a French term, derived from the theatre, meaning 'having been put into the scene'. In film, it involves the organisation of elements such as location, props, lighting and actors within the shot

montage sequence a rapidly edited sequence within a feature film. It can be used to indicate the passing of a long period of time, represent a process or introduce a location

non-diegetic music a film studies term for music on the soundtrack which does not come from a source within the film's narrative space

off-screen fixture a lighting source placed outside the frame which illuminates a shot

off-screen space space which is not seen but which is implied within a shot. Off-screen space is implied, for example, when a character walks into a shot

optical effect an editing device such as a fade or dissolve produced through processing in a laboratory

pan/panning short for 'panorama'. A camera movement where space is scanned from left to right or right to left

plot and story a theoretical distinction derived from the work of Russian formalist critics. The plot is the order in which story events are represented within a film's narrative. The story is the actual chronological order in which these events occurred. For example, the plot of a film about a murder investigation is likely to withhold full knowledge of the story until the murderer is revealed at the end. In terms of the story, however, the murder takes place at the beginning

point-of-view shot a shot approximating a character's visual point-of-view

practical an object within the frame which acts as a light source illuminating a shot

representation a theoretical term used in film, media and cultural studies, referring to images analysed as cultural constructions rather than realistic or accurate reflections

shallow focus one plane of action within the shot is focused whereas others are blurred

short-focal length lens a camera lens which distorts the shape and exaggerates the depth of what is within the frame

shot/reverse shot a standard convention for filming conversations.

cinematic terms

A framing and editing pattern which involves alternating shots of characters facing each other. All of the shots are filmed from the same side of a line between the characters

soft lighting   low intensity lighting which minimises contrasts between light and shade and shapes and textures within a shot

spectator   a film studies term describing the position constructed for the viewer by the film. This is different from the audience, the actual people who see the film

straight-on angle shot   a shot from a position looking straight at what is within the frame

tracking shot   a shot where the whole camera moves in any direction without leaving the ground. Tracking is often used to follow complex character movements or to move into a new space

zip pan   a rapid camera panning movement

credits

production company
Figment Film in association with
Noel Gay Motion Picture Company

director
Danny Boyle

producer
Andrew Macdonald

screenplay
John Hodge
(adapted from Irvine Welsh's novel)

director of photography
Brian Tufano

editor
Masahiro Hirakubo

art director
Tracey Gallacher

production designer
Kave Quinn

costume designer
Rachael Fleming

cast
Renton – Ewan McGregor
Spud – Ewen Bremner
Sick Boy – Jonny Lee Miller
Tommy – Kevin McKidd
Begbie – Robert Carlyle
Diane – Kelly MacDonald
Swanney – Peter Mullan
Mr Renton – James Cosmo
Mrs Renton – Eileen Nicholas
Allison – Susan Vidler
Lizzy – Pauline Lynch
Gail – Shirley Henderson
American tourist –
Stuart McQuarrie
Mikey Forrester – Irvine Welsh
Football commentator –
Archie MacPherson
Game show host – Dale Winton
Drug dealer – Keith Allen

music
Iggy Pop, 'Lust for Life'
Brian Eno, 'Deep Blue Day'
Primal Scream, 'Trainspotting'
Heaven 17, 'Temptation'
Sleeper, 'Atomic'
New Order, 'Temptation'
Iggy Pop, 'Nightclubbing'
Blur, 'Sing'
Lou Reed, 'Perfect Day'
Underworld, 'Dark and Long
(Dark Train Mix)'
Ice MC, 'Think about the Way'
Pulp, 'Mile End'
Bedrock featuring KYO,
'For What You Dream Of'
Elastica, '2:1'
Leftfield, 'A Final Hit'
Sleeper, 'Statuesque'
Underworld, 'Born Slippy'
Damon Albarn, 'Closet Romantic'